Suddenly DARK

Suddenly DARK

HUNTINGTON'S DISEASE:
My Family's Deadly Secret

GEORGE WILLIAM KNAUER

ARCHWAY
PUBLISHING

Archway Publishing books may be ordered through booksellers or by contacting:

Archway Publishing
1663 Liberty Drive
Bloomington, IN 47403
www.archwaypublishing.com
1 (888) 242-5904

Because of the dynamic nature of the Internet, any web addresses or links contained in this book may have changed since publication and may no longer be valid. The views expressed in this work are solely those of the author and do not necessarily reflect the views of the publisher, and the publisher hereby disclaims any responsibility for them.

Any people depicted in stock imagery provided by Thinkstock are models, and such images are being used for illustrative purposes only.
Certain stock imagery © Thinkstock.

ISBN: 978-1-4808-3012-7 (sc)
ISBN: 978-1-4808-3013-4 (e)

Print information available on the last page.

Archway Publishing rev. date: 4/7/2016

Dedication

I dedicate this book to my family, my friends,
and my community, Coxsackie, New York,
where I have lived for the past forty plus years
for helping me squeeze the lemons into lemonade.

Acknowledgements

I am very lucky to have beautiful friends like Marie DeFrancesco, Margaret Quigley and Anne Foster. They have helped and encouraged my writing. As a plumber I have always worked with tools. They have provided the tools I needed to write this book.

A retired English teacher, Marie became the can opener of the mind forcing me to empty out a life time of memories both good and bad. She spent countless hours helping me with typing and editing as we went along. Margaret has always been a positive, re-enforcing force from the beginning. She has been a pillar of strength for me. Anne was the one who insisted that I should start writing my life's story. She spent innumerable hours helping me recall my memories, typing and editing as we went along. I would also like to thank James Pollard for contributing his invaluable knowledge of Huntington's disease.

Victorious

George William Knauer

I shall not be a victim, but "victorious."
Death battled me almost to a draw.
It left my life but took my sight,
Leaving me as a knight to do battle
With life's uncertainties and fears.

Above my bed is a four-foot steel sword.
As I arise each morning with the crack of dawn,
And the sun creeps above the horizon,
The sun with its brightness
Refuses to penetrate my darkened eyes.
I grab my sword and put on my armor
To do battle each day.

With a tear rolling down my cheek,
As the warmth of the sun races across my face
Like the wind across a gentle meadow,
I go out into the world to do battle,
For I am a prisoner in my chamber of darkness.

I may not see the written word
Or all of the beauty God has put around us,
But that does not determine life for me to live.
From the depths of the deepest seas to the highest mountains,
From the arid deserts to the lush tropical forests,
There is as much beauty in what is unseen
as there is in what is seen.

There may be fear, there may be pain,
But it will not conquer, nor will it win.
In darkness there is light; there is fear, and there are tears.
I may stumble and fall on the rocky road of life,
But I will not quit, I will not fail,
Even though the darkness covers my day as it does my night.

I cannot die, for yet I have not succeeded.
There are things to be done,
There are words to be written,
There is a life to be lived.
For failure is not an option. I will be victorious.

Contents

Introduction

Now that I am in my mid-sixties and reflecting on my life so far, I realize it has been one hell of a journey. I don't blame any of my misfortunes on my family or childhood circumstances, including foster care from age two to seven, Wiltwyck School for Boys from eight to twelve, being returned to a house full of strangers, and a lifetime of dealing with Huntington's disease in my family. This book is about survival: a lifetime of dancing with the devil and not giving in to life's demons

Death, that miserable son of a bitch, has been chasing me since I was an infant. At eighteen months I was almost dead from pneumonia, dehydration, starvation, and weighing only eighteen pounds. At the age of ten, in the middle of winter, I fell into the low side of a dam and quickly sank to the bottom. Seconds before death, I was snatched from the frigid waters. At the age of twenty three, in a middle of a blinding snow storm, I drove off a fifty-foot cliff crashing through the frozen river and sinking to the bottom. Somehow I managed to get to shore. At the age of twenty seven, while headed home from a job with a little excess speed, I rounded a sharp corner. Ten feet before the railroad tracks, I heard the train's whistle. It was too late. I hit the lead engine broadside and bounced off three or four additional locomotives. When what was left of the truck finally came to rest, I was extricated. Death has continued to chase me over the past sixty-six years. In 2002, a critical event caused my near-death experience and total blindness. On August 5, 2006, I fell out a third floor window crashing onto the cement sidewalk below. I've been re-built with some extra screws, bolts, wires, and pipe. I will not let life-altering events get the better of me. God has a reason for keeping me here.

If there is anything I have learned, it is that you can't plan your life because it can change in a blink of an eye, or in my case, the blink of both eyes—FOREVER SUDDENLY DARK. Sit back, and let me start from the beginning.

1. Childhood/History

I wanted to write about my life from the beginning, but I have no memories of my own until the time I was placed in a foster home when I was about two years old. I don't remember the birth of a brother or a sister, being held by my mother and father, birthday parties, sibling rivalries, or as most people can recall, stories told by their parents. For the years before the age of eight, I have to rely on what I have gleaned from court records, documents, and conversations with older siblings. I want to thank my Aunt Tootsie (Evelyn) who at eighty-four was invaluable in putting this together.

My mother, Lillian Beuscher, was born on September 8, 1919 in Brooklyn, New York of Herman and Aurelia Walker Beuscher. She was one of six children: four girls and two boys. I will give you a little of her family history because it will help to make sense of what happened later in my family and my life. Through court records I have been able to trace back to approximately 1810 to my maternal great-great grandparents. My grandmother Aurelia died in Creedmoor State Hospital (an insane asylum) in 1937 of what is now known as Huntington's disease. She had been diagnosed as having psychosis with mental deficiency. Her brother went to the psychiatric hospital in Poughkeepsie New York. My great grandmother was known to clean one day and live in filth and disorder for the next six months. She had an explosive temper and irrational behavior patterns. Up until the 1950's, before Huntington's disease was identified, people with these conditions were institutionalized and considered crazy or mentally deficient. Their erratic movements often made them appear to be stumbling drunk.

My father, Arthur Jack Knauer Sr., was born on March 25, 1914 in Brooklyn, New York. His parents were Jacob and Mary Odell Knauer, born in New York City. He was one of eleven children: seven boys and four girls.

My father had known my mother for two years before they married but had no idea of her family history. My parents were married in the Lutheran Church in Brooklyn, New York in 1940. They had seven children.

On October 8, 1941, less than a year after they married, my father volunteered and entered the U. S. Army in the 308th Engineering Battalion, 83rd Division. At Camp Atterbury in Indiana, he attended school to become a baker and cook. He served in Central Europe, Normandy, Northern France, and the Rhineland between April 1944 and July 1945. He was honorably discharged as Calvary Staff Sergeant on September 12, 1945. He never spoke about his military service to his country and the hell that he had seen in the war. His sister, Aunt Tootsie, told me that when his brothers, like my father, came back from World War II, they never talked about what they had been through, and they began drinking heavily. Another of his brothers, my namesake George Knauer, was in Tokyo when Japan surrendered.

After the war, my father worked in a bronze and lead casting factory. Two years after their marriage, their first child Kathleen was born in 1942, Arthur in 1943, Rosemary in 1946, and John in 1947. I was born on April 16, 1949. Lillian was born in 1950, and Robert in 1952. Robert passed on October 21, 2004 and John on March 26, 2006, both from Huntington's disease, Lillian passed shortly after birth. Mother having seven children over a ten-year period and her increasing loss of mental and physical abilities, were the impetus for the courts to become involved.

Our family was very poor. In fact, we grew up on the dirty side of "dirt poor." We lived in a Brooklyn "walk-up" apartment at 846 Gates Avenue. My father's sister, Aunt Eleanor, and her husband, Uncle Pete, lived upstairs, and my mother's sister, Aunt Tootsie and Uncle John lived downstairs. This was before electric refrigerators were common; the ice man would go through the city streets delivering blocks of ice. Rent was about $18.00 a month.

Evenings, either Mom or Dad would go upstairs to Aunt Eleanor and Uncle Pete's, or they would come down to our apartment, and they would drink and play cards all night. Weekends were the same way—along about midday, our aunts and uncles got together and drank all weekend. Kathleen doesn't ever remember seeing them together when they were not drinking. Our aunts and uncles were heavy beer drinkers, but they all got along and had a good time together.

My sister Kathleen remembers my mother being sick a lot. There were days when she could not get out of bed, and Aunt Eleanor or Uncle Pete would come down and make sure we were okay.

One of our neighbors made an anonymous call to the Brooklyn Society for the Prevention of Cruelty to Children because of my parents' inability to provide a clean living environment and adequate food. This had also happened to my mother's mother and my grandmother's mother. A social worker came and reviewed my family's living conditions. The social worker reported that our home of four rooms was indescribably filthy and foul smelling. The beds were without linens and infested with vermin. Beer bottles were used in lieu of baby bottles. Papers, garbage, and debris were scattered about the floors. My brothers, sisters, and I were thin and appeared to be under-nourished. Both of my parents were interviewed by the Protection Agency. According to the report, they were of limited intelligence, my mother more limited than my father. The report also said that "they were cooperative to a degree." Under supervision of the agency, a fair improvement was noted in home conditions. The rooms were painted and new linoleum was laid in the kitchen. During this time, my youngest sister, Lillian was born at home without the aid of a midwife or doctor. She was not even taken to the Clinic for a checkup.

Even with follow up visits, our home environment soon reverted back into the former deplorable conditions. My mother seemed to be even more confused and over burdened with her responsibilities, but she did not wish to have her children placed. My father worked and could give my mother very little assistance in the home. The Society for the Prevention of Cruelty to Children again filed a Neglect Petition on March 20, 1950 alleging that my parents were improper guardians for their six children—that they failed to provide a proper home, to keep the children clean, or to provide adequate medical care for them. Subsequent visits to the home showed no improvement. A finding of Neglect was made.

My youngest sister Lillian, who was born on August 3, 1950,

was found dead on October 16, 1950 (three months old) of malnutrition. The police came to our home due to Lillian's death, and this was the impetus for the state to remove all of the remaining children. It was not my mother's fault. Irrational behaviors such as this are part of the inherited disease. In fact, my grandmother had unintentionally caused the death of her first child.

The authorities were particularly concerned about me because I was eighteen months old and weighed only eighteen pounds, suffering from malnutrition and unable to sit up or walk. They took me away immediately. I was placed in the Greenpoint Hospital in Brooklyn on October 16, 1950. However, after a short stay in the hospital, my mother, against doctor's orders, removed me from the hospital. The next day, my parents took the rest of their children to Brooklyn Family Court. The court then sent them to Kings County Hospital for an examination and medical care. A physical and psychiatric examination was ordered for my mother and father.

On January 29, 1952, we children were placed in temporary shelters: Kathleen was nine years, eight months old, Arthur was seven years, eleven months old, Rosemary was five years, six months old, John was four years, two months old, and I was two years, nine months old. At this point I was returned to Greenpoint Hospital until I was healthy enough to be placed in a foster home. (This was the beginning of my being moved from place to place, never having a stable home until I was fourteen and I moved in with Charlie Hancock, my life-long friend. It was the first time that I had what I consider "parents", Betty and Bob Hancock. Charlie's sisters Nancy and Bonnie and brother Bob also accepted me into their family. I have also been an 'uncle' to all subsequent generations.) When we went back to court in March 1952, Kathy and Artie were placed by one agency in two different foster homes, while Rosemary and John were placed by another agency into the same home for a short period of time. My brothers and sisters were placed in Ozone Park, New York so they could see each other. My father's great Aunt Eva lived nearby and every few months they would all go to her house. My father, and sometimes my mother, would visit. We were told that these were temporary foster homes and that our mother needed to see a doctor.

On Tuesday, October 30, 1952, Robert was born at home without the assistance of a nurse or midwife. My father decided to hide Robert from Family Court so that he would not be removed as his other children had been. However, he and his sisters feared that the baby would not survive under my mother's care because of her diminishing mental and physical capabilities. Previously, her youngest daughter had died of starvation and neglect. Two days after his birth, my father brought Robert to be cared for by my Aunt Tootsie and Uncle John who lived in the downstairs apartment. Robert lived with her for approximately nine months until my mother called the police, saying that Aunt Tootsie had stolen her baby. My aunt said she would have raised Robert as her own but decided against that idea after the police came. Robert was then raised by Aunt Eleanor for the next two years. Aunt Eleanor lived in the apartment above my father.

On December 8, 1953, my older brother, Arthur was placed with Wiltwyck School for Boys in Esopus, New York. Later, John and I also attended, at different intervals, the same school. I didn't even know that either one of my brothers existed until I was reunited in 1961 with my father.

On March 30, 1954, Judge Kaplan officially and permanently

committed four of the children (Kathleen, Rosemary, John, and me) to the Department of Welfare because our mother's health had not improved and my parents were still unable to provide suitable living conditions. We were not to be returned until approximately the age of twelve with hopes that they would then be able to take care of their children. Robert, who was hidden from the Court, remained at home with my father. Because his other children had been removed from his care, my father took special care of Robert.

My sister Kathleen and I were with Windham Children's Services; Rosemary and John were at Brooklyn Bureau of Social Services. In November 1954, at the age of five, I was at a foster home at 114-39 132nd Street, Ozone Park, New York, where I stayed until the spring of 1958 when I was placed at Wiltwyck School for Boys situated in the mid-Hudson Valley. All that I remember of going to the foster home was that there were strange people and I was told that this was going to be my home. I remember climbing up on the couch and looking out the window, crying as the car that had brought me began to drive away. The house was on a tree-lined street at the end of a cul-de-sac. I remember no leaves on the trees and the sky being overcast.

I seem to have blocked most of my other memories from this period of my life. I clearly recall being hit with a strap, being hungry, and sleeping three in a bed. We picked our clothes in the morning from what we had piled at the end of the bed the night before. I have had flashbacks throughout my life of abuse—both sexual and physical. It was a gut-wrenching decision to write about it. I've never spoken about this in sixty-six years. This secret has haunted many of my marriages and relationships with other women. This will be the last mention of it.

After consulting with doctors who believed that "good country air" would help my mother, my father moved to Pine Bush in the Catskills in 1953. The court did not consider it advisable to release us children to his care when he moved from Brooklyn to up-state New York.

My father worked for a man named George Kline. He and my father had grown up together; one made big money and the other just got by. When George Kline found out that my mother was ill, he bought an old three-story, block-long building and set up a satellite foundry in Pine Bush to help my father get my mother out of the city. My father became the foreman and shop manager of Sellright Gift Corporation's up-state branch, a lead foundry that made lead and brass figurines.

My father got things set up with the business and purchased a home, planning to have Robert and my mother join him. Before they were able to come, my father left his dog (whose name was "Dog") in the basement of the house whenever he visited my mother and Robert in the city. During one of the visits, he left a kerosene lantern burning in the basement. Apparently, "Dog" knocked the lantern over and the brown, two-story house on Maple Avenue burned to the ground. Luckily, nobody was home, but the dog was lost.

My father had no insurance on the house. Once again, George Kline came to the rescue. He purchased a house on the corner of Maple and Depot Streets for them to live in.

I've been told by one of my uncles that my parents couldn't even catch a break when they moved their belongings to the country. My father and his brother had to get out and push the truck up some of the mountainous roads to Pine Bush, as the truck had trouble with all the weight inside.

Pine Bush was a small, sleepy village. My father lived and worked all within three blocks. He lived on the corner of one block, worked in the middle block, and drank at Herman's Bar in the third block. There was a small town grocery and general store in the middle of the town and a single gas station. He never drove a car; he walked from home to work, to the bar and home. Even though he enjoyed a liquid lunch and usually had a beer in his hand, he was never stumbling drunk or violent. Funny, many years later, here I am, like my father, living in a small village on its main street, just me and my dog Charlie.

Soon after they arrived in Pine Bush, my mother was seen by Dr. Weiss in Ellenville, New York who brought in a specialist from the Neurological Institute. Dr. John H. Taterka of New York City reported that he thought that they were dealing with an organic neurological disease of a degenerative type. The basal ganglia and, probably, cerebellar tracts appeared to be involved. He said that a correct classification of this condition was not possible without further studies.

I recently wrote to Jim Pollard, a world-renowned authority on Huntington's disease, to ask him if what the doctor reported is typical of the onset of Huntington's. He wrote back as follows:

> I wouldn't say that it's "typical" but it would fit a profile of early Huntington's disease. There are some signs that he notes that are movement related. But the cognitive symptoms often appear first. He doesn't note any beyond referring to the problems that she has caring for you kids. So they were clearly evident, but he did not do any cognitive testing. Back then he wouldn't have

anyway, most of the neuropsychological tests have been
developed in the subsequent years.

By Dr. Weiss's recommendation, my mother was seen at
Letchworth Village Out-Patient Clinic by Dr. Jervis in July 1954.
She was diagnosed with Huntington's Chorea and became a resident
of Letchworth Developmental Disability Services in Thiells, New
York on February 8, 1955. My father was told she would gradually
become worse and eventually lose her mind and control of her body.
My father never told any of us that our mother had Huntington's
disease or what her illness was. My older sister Kathleen told me
that she thought she had Multiple Sclerosis.

Huntington's disease is a mind and body destroying disease
which never skips a generation. My maternal grandmother, Aurelia
Walker Beuscher, died at the age of 45 from Huntington's. Her
mother also died of the disease. Huntington's disease affects the
brain in the same way that a tiny bruise affects a grapefruit. That
pin-point bruise grows larger and larger until the fruit is rotten.
Huntington's affects the motor control part of the brain causing the
wild and erratic movements of limbs which is called the Chorea (the
dance). Until it was described in a medical journal by Dr. George
Huntington in the 1870's, it was referred to as "Chorea" because of
the erratic movements of the limbs which characterize the disease.
It also affects the body's metabolism which speeds up, leading to
massive weight loss. One's ability to articulate degenerates as the
disease progresses, leaving the patient sometimes angry and frustrated because he or she cannot be understood. Either pneumonia
or heart failure facilitates the end.

My efforts to adequately explain Huntington's disease fall

short. The disease is best explained by an expert, so I asked Jim Pollard, a renowned specialist in this disease, to explain my mother's condition. This is what he wrote:

"Hi, George,

As promised here are some notes I made while I was reading your Mom's history. I've included lots of things, just random thoughts, in case you find them interesting.

It appears that the onset of your Mom's cognitive disorder predated the onset of her movement disorder. This is always hard to tell, especially looking back 50 years. However, your Dad did "insist" that she had "no outward physical signs of illness" when he acknowledged changes in her temper with yelling and demands. Based on stories, this is consistent with both John and Robert's onset. Correct me if I'm mistaken. This is interesting although it's clearly not the rule.

When I see that neighbors complained about her neglecting you guys and that your Dad hadn't noticed it, I'm not surprised. Interestingly, Woody Guthrie tells the same story about his Mom in *Bound for Glory*. She was much worse with tantrums when his Dad wasn't home. He and his brother Roy would also try to put the house back together before their Dad got home to protect her from his father's knowing about the tantrums and yelling and screaming. Their neighbors, too, apparently knew what was going on and its seriousness before Woody's Dad did. Similarly, Jerry Guthrie was sympathetic to his wife's plight just like your Dad was when it was reported to social service agencies.

When Moms with Huntington's disease neglect the cleanliness of their kids, it's no surprise. Most people with Huntington's disease hate or avoid showers and bathing themselves, never mind their kids! And the "deplorable conditions" of the home are no more than the cognitive deficit showing itself in the inability to "organize" cleaning up the house. Think of it. Cleaning up is a relatively complex task, as simple as it appears. It involves reviewing what goes where, what's dirty enough to wash, what needs laundering, what goes into the garbage as well as sweeping, wiping down, doing dishes, cooking, and God knows what else. It gets so confusing, you just don't do it. The reference in the court documents to spaghetti and rice pudding may have just been a lack of judgment. I suspect this could have happened with a pantry full of groceries too.

When Dr. Weiss said she would "gradually get worse and eventually lose her mind," he knew she had Huntington's disease. That's why she was seen by the specialist from the Neurological Institute. We can presume he was a neurologist. This is where they realized she had a neurological disorder and didn't have just a "mental illness." Speculating now, this decision may have kept her out of the state psychiatric hospital in Poughkeepsie. Perhaps since it was a neurological condition, they thought Letchworth, primarily an institution for folks with mental retardation, was more appropriate. I bet it was a better option for her.

How times have changed! "Moron" was a legitimate diagnosis of mental retardation used by the medical community back then. At Letchworth you can really see that her Huntington's disease became more pronounced with increased balance problems, jerky movements, and slurred speech.

I'm sure lousy dental condition doesn't surprise you! It seems to follow everyone with Huntington's disease. And in those days, 1955, all institutions removed even teeth with minor problems."

Jim mentioned my mother's having been diagnosed as a "moron." When I read this term in her medical records, I was stunned. I think of that as a derogatory word, an insult. I asked Jim for some clarification. He told me that from the early 1800's through the late nineteen-fifties "moron," "imbecile," and "idiot" were terms used to describe certain mental deficiencies. "Moron" would have described someone with mental capacity comparable to that of a person between eight and fifteen years old. These terms fell out of use as the terms began to be used to insult people. They were replaced by "mild," "moderate," "severe," and "profound retardation." Jim said that today she would be labeled as moderately retarded.

Back to the story. Herman, my father's co-worker, and his wife Thelma lived next door to the shop. Thelma helped raise Robert as an infant until Kathleen was returned from foster care in 1957. At the age of fifteen, she began to take care of Robert when she was not in school. She did the best she could.

Each of us, except Rosemary, was brought home around the age of twelve. Shortly after my mother's death, I was returned home from Wiltwyck and united with my father, brothers, and sister. It was hard suddenly having siblings (Kathleen, Arthur, John, and Robert) and making the emotional connections. I didn't know I had another sister, Rosemary, until 1962. It was traumatic leaving a structured environment and going to utter chaos. I did not know when we were going to eat, when my father was going to be sober, or when my older sister was going to fly off the handle.

The oldest of us boys, Arthur, went to Wiltwyck School for Boys before me. He went into the army October 20, 1960 while I was at Wiltwyck. I did not meet him until he was home on leave during the summer of 1962. He married Dorothy on December 22, 1962. I remember three things about Arthur's wedding. First, he caught me, age twelve, smoking a cigar and decided to cure me of the habit. He proceeded to make me eat it. The cure did not work. I still have a love affair with good cigars. If I can't smoke a cigar and ride my Harley in heaven, I am not going. Second, I had an embarrassing haircut. Kathy and Art thought that my hair was not suitable for the wedding and ganged up on me with a pair of dull scissors. In order to cover the bald spots, I was the only one at the church service wearing a hat. The third thing was that I learned I had another sister. Rosemary was then 16 years old. This was also the first time that she had seen our father since she was about six years old.

Rosemary was never returned home. My father felt that she was settled in with a loving foster family. She had been doing well in school and had a future. I think it took more love to leave her in that environment rather than bringing her home to abject poverty, alcoholism, and our ever present Mr. & Mrs. Cockroach and their extended family. She later got married and had three children. She turned out to be a great mother and lady. To this day, she considers her foster parents her mother and father.

I have asked Rosemary if she remembers that wedding. She remembers mostly thinking how strange it felt to meet people that were supposed to be family. She wrote the following:

> I was sitting in the living room waiting for someone when I felt someone watching me. As I looked up, Dad was there and he said, "Don't blame your Mother for what happened." Maybe a little harshly, I replied, "I don't blame her as she was a victim, just like her children." He walked away. I wanted to just go but Kathy insisted that I say goodbye to him. It was like saying goodbye to a stranger and I never saw him again. When I was getting on the bus, Kathy grabbed my arm and said, "Dad said that you are your mother's daughter, you have her spirit." It was weird to hear that because my case worker said that my father always described me as "her mother's daughter." Not sure if he meant that in a good or negative way.

Rosemary was the only one of us children to ever see our mother after the court ordered separation. Her case worker took her to see her at Letchworth on November 5, 1960. Rosemary was fourteen at the time and only remembers her being "sick," but not the nature of her illness. It was a short visit. Mother died six months later.

Soon after Arthur's wedding, I moved in with Charlie and his family, the Hancock's. To this day, we are still best of friends and I am still very much part of his family. We are like brothers.

My Aunt Dotty (nee Dorothy Frances Locks) married my Uncle Harold (Harry) Knauer, she sent the following letter regarding my mother.

Dear George,

Not too much I can tell you about your Mom! She was pretty with dark hair and eyes. She was about five ft seven inches tall and nice build. Was pregnant most of the time, when she had Robert is when I noticed she was not steady on her feet. They thought she was drunk but your mother never drank to my knowledge. I lost track of family after they moved and I went to work for Abraham & Strauss where I worked for twenty five years.

Your father worked in Wassaic State School, Amenia, Dutchess County New York. Enlisted in the U. S. Calvery on October 8, 1941 at Camp Upton.

The only time I was in your house in Pine Bush was when Arthur got married. Most times, when Aunt

Emma and Uncle Lou and me and Uncle Harry went up, we spent the day in the bar. That is where your Dad would be. He never spoke of your Mom or told us where she was. When she was young, she worked as a domestic aide. I think all of you kids were born in New York.

Wish I could tell you more. Take care.

Love,
Aunt Dotty

2. Wiltwyck School for Boys

The Wiltwyck School for Boys in Esopus, New York, on the opposite side of the Hudson River from the Roosevelt's family home, first opened its doors to African-American juvenile delinquents in 1936. The school, under the leadership of the Episcopal City Mission Society, experienced some initial success at treating the troubled youngsters who attended, most of whom had grown up in undesirable and neglected sections of New York City. However, by 1942 Wiltwyck suffered from such a severe lack of funds that it was in danger of closing.

In 1942, several remarkable women, particularly the First Lady, Eleanor Roosevelt, helped reorganize the school and joined its board of directors. Mrs. Roosevelt, a former teacher, had been moved by the courage that the Wiltwyck Academy had shown in taking an interest in underprivileged African-American children and immediately wanted to help in any way that she could. That same year Wiltwyck ended its affiliation with the Protestant church and became an interracial treatment center for young boys between the ages of eight and twelve.

The above information on Wiltwyck School for Boys was from The Eleanor Roosevelt Papers Project, a university-chartered research center associated with the Department of History of the George Washington University, Washington, DC.

In a fundraising letter written on December 3, 1945, Eleanor Roosevelt wrote:

"In their short lives they have experienced more tragedy than most adults experience during a lifetime. They are victims of all the hostilities and maladjustments New York City's slums can foster. They come to the school at Esopus, NEW YORK—the only school of its kind—from the Children's Courts of the City of New York and stay until they are rehabilitated, usually a period from six months to two years (later becoming a four year school).

Under an interracial Board and staff Wiltwyck School offers these children an atmosphere of warmth and understanding—a home. The boys improve in health, learn to like school, and catch up with their school work. They have become skilled in constructive activities and learn to live cooperatively with others. By these means they gain the self-confidence that will enable them to cope with the realities of living."

Because a significant portion of the school's budget came from private donations, Mrs. Roosevelt's role in raising money for the academy was crucial to its survival. It was a task that she remained wedded to for the rest of her life, even up until her last months in 1962 when she busied herself soliciting monies to relocate the academy to Yorktown Heights, New York. The school itself managed to survive for another nineteen years after Roosevelt's death, but was finally forced to close its doors in 1981 due, ultimately, to a lack of money.

It is at Wiltwyck School that my memories of youth begin. During the years that Mrs. Roosevelt was associated with Wiltwyck, it was very different from the reform schools of the present. There were no chain link fences, gates, or barbed wire to imprison the boys at the school. The school had very basic classes in reading, writing and arithmetic. It was run very lovingly. We had good food, movies every week, horses, and a large camping cabin up in the mountains where we would spend a week each summer roasting marshmallows, telling ghost stories, and having fun. Sometimes when we went to bed, one of the counselors would have hidden in the rafters, keeping very quiet until we were asleep, and then he would let out a loud scream. We were terribly frightened but enjoyed the experience. We learned to fish, swim, ride horses, clean the stalls, and groom the horses. If any of us did something we were not supposed to do, our punishment might be missing our next rotation with the horses, forfeiting our swimming time at the lake, or losing our week at the cabin.

The horse barn was a large, two-story, gray stone building with a large clock tower covered in ivy. The building was like a medieval castle, about three or four hundred feet long, very foreboding and intriguing to a young boy. It had a large twenty-foot wide ramp where we would lead the horses in and out. We kids used to play up in the hay loft which was a very large, cavernous play ground.

I remember once running through the hay loft, not looking, and hitting a big old beam knocking myself out cold.

Each year, we boys were taken, in groups of approximately fifteen, to the Franklin D. Roosevelt Library and Museum where we had the run of the grounds. One group went on Saturday and the other on Sunday. Later we went to Val Kill, Mrs. Roosevelt's home, where she would put on picnics consisting of a smorgasbord of food, far in excess of what we ever got at Wiltwyck, including hot dogs, hamburgers, watermelon, and chips. After playing and eating, we were gathered on the tennis court. At this time, Mrs. Roosevelt would come out, her frail body dressed in black, her white hair in sharp contrast. We did not realize that she was the former First Lady; to us she was just a kind old woman who would come out at the last part of the day and for an hour or more read us Rudyard Kipling stories. As she approached us on the tennis court, you could hear a dime drop and tell if it was heads or tails. From Mrs. Roosevelt, I learned the joy of being read a story. The memory of her reading to us is forever seared in my mind.

There were two counselors at the school whose names were Mr. Nixon and Mr. Kennedy, the same as the candidates for the presidency in 1959. That year our teachers used this coincidence to teach us about elections. The counselors "campaigned," each trying to persuade us that he was the better choice. We voted by paper ballot and Mr. Nixon won. This was my first civics lesson.

Our housing was an old converted monastery. The building was in the shape of a horse shoe with two wings. Our sleeping quarters were the outer branches of the wings. There were four or five bunk beds in each room with foot lockers for storage. One of the main contributions Mrs. Roosevelt brought to Wiltwyck

School was equipment. Our beds were military bunk beds, our blankets were printed with "US Army," and the horses were from the Army's Calvary division when they were phased out and the army switched to mechanized machinery. The military-like living structure instilled in me a habit of cleanliness and organization which has followed me through the rest of my life.

In the right wing were small class rooms each accommodating eight to ten students. There was also an administrative office, a nurse's office, and an infirmary. The inner left side was the gym. The gym had little equipment. There was a boxing ring in the center of the room. We would run laps around it and do calisthenics. We learned to box. If there were any disputes, the boxing ring was where we were taken to settle them.

On a little hill to the left of the entrance to the school grounds was a trailer which housed the psychologists. Each student was assigned a guidance counselor and we would go to "The Hill" weekly for counseling or to see if there were any problems that they could help us with.

On the right was a long building which housed the dining room. On Sunday, it was turned into a chapel. The services were non-denominational. On Saturday nights, it functioned as a movie theatre. I remember there were a lot of Westerns and pirate movies. Afterwards, we would play "cowboys and Indians" or "pirates." When I was almost twelve, my guidance counselor asked me if I thought that I was a little too old to be playing "cowboys and Indians." The answer I gave her was, "I live among the boys. If I don't play…. What am I? Too good for them? If I do play, you think I'm not maturing." I felt like I was caught between a rock and a hard place.

It was in the gym at Wiltwyck that a very thin, young boy, who had been beat on occasionally, learned to box. This young boy went on to become the Heavy Weight Champion of the World—Mr. Floyd Patterson. He was held up to us as a role model.

On July 21, 1960, I and another young boy were invited to the Hotel Commodore in New York City to witness Mr. Floyd Patterson receiving the Heavy Weight Championship crown. Before the dinner, we went to see the premier of the movie *Ben Hur*. We were seated in the very front row. When the chariots raced around the Coliseum, they came towards us—we swore they were coming at us off the screen, and we ran up the exit aisle!

The testimonial dinner was co-chaired by Jackie Robinson and Ed Sullivan, with the proceeds going for the benefit of the Wiltwyck School. Cus D'Amato, who was Patterson's trainer and who later trained Mike Tyson, presented Mr. Patterson with a fourteen-karat gold crown set with one hundred seventy-four diamonds, two hundred forty-eight rubies and sapphires and two hundred fifty pearls. He also received a ceremonial robe sent by the president of Ghana.

One thing stands out in my mind about that dinner at the Hotel Commodore: the array of knives, forks, and spoons at our place settings. As the appetizer was put in front of us, not knowing what an appetizer was, we looked up at the Wiltwyck School counselor that accompanied us, and asked in amazement, "Can we eat the dessert now?"

When we saw Floyd Patterson crowned the Heavy Weight Champion of the World, I didn't realize the magnitude of his achievement. But seeing someone from the same school as myself gave me the idea that we could become anything we wanted to by working hard and staying focused.

Amazingly, this is not the end of the story; some fifty years later a friend of mine named Vince Schettini invited me to join him and his father Mario to a little coffee shop across the street. Mario was also blind. It wasn't until the passing of Mario Schettini who was a jeweler, did his son Vince learn that he was mistaken about his father's putting the jewels on the heavy weight championship belt. Shortly afterward, I told Vince about what his father had really done, as I witnessed the crown being placed on Floyd Patterson's head with the jewels his father had installed on the crown.

Another special occasion was when Harry Belafonte came to Wiltwyck School. He showed us how to take fifty-five gallon drums, cut them, and fashion them into Caribbean-style drums. Using a punch, the center was divided into sections of varied heights and then polished until it shined. With talented hands, music was produced.

At Wiltwyck School there was an apple orchard bordering the school's property. We would climb over the wall to steal apples. The farmer, to persuade us not to steal his apples, would replace the pellets in buck-shot shells with rock salt. It would take many months to heal our behinds, and we stole no more apples.

I learned how to drive my first car at Wiltwyck on Black Hawk Road. One of the guidance counselors was brave enough to teach us how to drive.

Fishing at Wiltwyck was so much fun. The first and only time I ever went fishing, we did not have fishing poles, so we used baseball bats. The Esopus Creek was so overrun with fish that we just took the bats and beat the hell out of the water. The kids downstream would catch the stunned fish with nets. The "nets" were screens taken from the dorm windows. Bet'cha it's the one and only time that anyone will ever hear of someone fishing with a baseball bat.

We swam in a man-made lake fed by a stream. In the spring, we would slide boards into a permanent fixture to dam up the lake, and in the fall we would remove the boards. It seemed funny to be swimming in the lake at one time of the year, when at another time of year, we could walk on the bottom of the lake as it reverted back to a narrow but steady stream.

Once in a while someone would run away. I don't think we knew where we were going or why. Something in our minds just told us to run away. Needless to say, we never succeeded and were always returned to the school. I ran away from the school twice. The first time was on a winter's day. The water that had run over the spillway of the dam carved a deep pool of standing water. Walking on what was left of the dam, I fell into that icy water. I was drowning. It was a very peaceful, surreal experience until out of nowhere a counselor appeared and yanked me from the water. Perhaps he had been watching me all of the time to see what I was up to. It was one of many times I have been saved from dying.

I ran away again that same winter. As I look back, I realize I was not a very bright young man. I seemed to run away in the winter. I never thought about doing it in the spring, summer, or fall when the weather was nice. This time I made it across the dam. There was a set of railroad tracks between the lake and the summer cabin. Having no idea where they went, I simply started to walk along the tracks. I was ten years old, short, and very puny. As I continued to walk, it began to snow. The heavy snow accumulated quickly. Soon it was a white out and I was waist high in snow, struggling with each step. Suddenly a farmer appeared, picked me up, and carried me to his house where his wife got me out of my frozen clothes and wrapped me in a blanket. She then gave me lunch of soup, a sandwich, and hot chocolate. Eventually, she washed and dried my clothes. Later in the day, her husband took me back to the school in his truck. When I got back to school I expected an ass-whooping, but it was as if I'd never left. There was no punishment. A counselor sat me down and talked to me in a reassuring voice asking me why I'd left and where I thought I was going. The next time I thought about running away, I realized there was no purpose to it. I had no place to go and no one to go to.

My experience was not unusual. Whenever we boys ran away or tried to, anybody within twenty miles of the school would take care of us, give us something to eat, and eventually return us safely. Neighbors around the school were as caring as the counselors that ran the school. It was a joyous thing to realize that people cared for and about us.

My first female guidance counselor was matronly like the other women at Wiltwyck who worked as teachers, nurses, and office staff. I was maybe ten or eleven when I got a new guidance counselor named Maryanne. She was platinum blond and wore form-fitting dresses. It seemed that she just enjoyed teasing young boys. She would often unbutton the top three buttons of her blouse saying how hot it was in there, exposing a considerable amount of cleavage. I spent more time fantasizing what was under her tight, red dress than on her questions and answers about my mental or physical well-being. It was rather embarrassing being ten or eleven and standing in front of her desk with an erection. I always had to retreat to the bathroom before leaving her office. That was my first experience with masturbation. I was considered lucky to be assigned to her. Many of the other boys would try to trade time slots with me. Oh yes, I never missed a weekly visit with Maryanne.

It was then that I first started looking at women in a different fashion. I was confused. There was June Cleaver and Harriet Nelson, and on the other hand, there was a guidance counselor who could melt butter forty feet away with the body she had. I guess that is where a lifetime of being attracted to older women began.

Another memorable moment occurred when I was in the infirmary recovering from having my tonsils removed. The nurse pointed out the window and said to me, "There goes your father and brother." I will never forget that image, a man wearing khaki pants and a brown leather jacket walking away holding the hand of a small boy. I tried to call to him but I had no voice. Nothing came out. I had no idea who the boy was. I didn't know at that time that I had any siblings.

One warm, sunny summer day when I was about ten, I decided to take a nap on a long high stone wall that had a flat slate top. While I was taking my nap, a small group of yellow jackets crawled up the leg of my shorts and decided to take up residence in a very warm and intimate place. When I began to stir and awaken, those yellow jackets took great umbrage at their home being moved and began to sting the living hell out of my most delicate of body parts. I proceeded to rip off my shorts and streak across the campus screaming until I jumped into a nearby creek. Subsequently, I spent several days recovering in the infirmary. An extraordinary and memorable moment for a ten year old boy!

We were kept busy at Wiltwyck and life was not unpleasant. However, I had a sense that something was missing. There was a void in my life and I often went off alone, a behavior that I have continued to this day. It was at one of these times, sitting up on a hill overlooking the lake and castle where we rode horses, that I lost a tooth. The last time I told the nurse I had pain, my tonsils were removed, and thus I did not mention the pain in my mouth. I was very surprised when the tooth came out. I hid the tooth and told no one.

On April 21 1961, I was pulled aside by a counselor and told that my mother had died. I hadn't a clue what she was talking about. I had no idea what a real family was because up to that point foster homes and guidance counselors at Wiltwyck were my family. I didn't know what I should feel when she said, "Your mother is dead." At that time I was void of emotion.

When I returned to class, one of the boys asked me, "What's up?" I told him that my mother had died. He asked me, "Aren't you going to cry?" Never having known my mother or even what a mother was, I did not know how to react to her death. Between eighteen months and the seventh year of my life, I had been in a succession of foster homes. I had no idea what a "normal" family was until that summer when I was reunited with my father and my brothers and sisters.

In 1996, I had a chance encounter at Hyde Park, Franklin D. Roosevelt's home, with a curator who overheard me talking to a friend about Wiltwyck School and Eleanor Roosevelt's involvement with the school. I was asked if I would be willing to be interviewed about this. This interview was filmed for the Eleanor Roosevelt archives and a copy resides in the Library of Congress.

3. Youth

It was in the Wiltwyck School's charter that, at the age of twelve, boys would be returned to their biological families, if possible. In 1961, I was brought to Pine Bush, New York and introduced to my father, my three brothers (Art, John, and Robert) and one of my two sisters (Kathleen). When I met them, there was no emotional connection. There was no hugging, laughing, or crying. We became five strangers living in the same house, a group of individuals with the same last name, but not a family. Even to this day we are very distant.

Pine Bush was a very small community. Everything was within a two-block radius. It was one of those towns with a single red light and everyone knew each other—a Norman Rockwell type town. A few hours after arriving home, I was allowed to go out and play. It's hard to believe at twelve years old I could get lost in four square blocks, but I did.

We lived over the hardware store on Main Street almost across from the City Hall. We had to go up the outside of the building on a metal fire escape to enter our apartment. When we went in and turned the lights on, I saw thousands of cockroaches. I had never seen one before. Eventually we moved, but somehow those cockroaches seemed to move with us. My run-ins with cockroaches had a profound effect on me. After I left my father's house, I was determined never to live like that again. I will work and play in dirt, but I sure will not live in it.

My father was emotionally withdrawn, an island unto himself. In the early morning, he would get up and have his cup of instant Maxwell House coffee. He'd read the paper and talk to his parakeets. During the early morning hours he was sometimes approachable and took the time to talk with me. This was the only time that he did. The conversation, however, was limited to trivialities. He never spoke of my mother or his past, and I dared not ask. From the time he left the house until the next morning he was a stranger.

His days were ritualized. During the first summer, I worked with him at the foundry where he was the foreman. He was very quiet, sitting at his work station soldering in the air holes in the lead figurines and constantly smoking a Camel cigarette. Periodically, he would walk up to the front of the shop, stand quietly isolated, and smoke another cigarette. At 4:30 P.M. he went to Herman's Bar for his Schaefer Beer and dinner. Then he would come home, sit in his chair in the living room, and have more beer. He was again very quiet, as if in his own world. Sundays from two to five would find him taking an afternoon nap.

My father, five foot, six inches and about 170 pounds, had not one gray hair on his head. He had an extremely strong right hand from picking up what they call "pigs." Pigs are solid lead bars weighing over one hundred pounds. He put them into a smelter where they were melted into a liquid form from which they made lead castings. He had broken the center knuckle on his right hand and the knuckle had inverted to the palm of his hand. His hand had been burned many times by splatters from putting "pigs" into the melting pot and was white with scar tissue. If we did something wrong, he would catch us with that right hand.

If one of us had done something wrong and he had clocked the wrong one by mistake, he would say, "Well, that was for the trouble you were in that I missed." If we had been punished at school for something we did wrong and came home complaining about the teacher swatting us, he would hit us again. It took only one swat for me to learn to keep my mouth shut about my school antics. He was very rigid in how he approached life. He would say, "My house, my rules." Every once in a while, when he had too much to drink, he became aggressive and confrontational. He would say, "If you boys think you are man enough—bring it on." Once, John decided to take him up on the challenge. I caught my brother and pummeled his ass. If my friend Charlie hadn't been there, I would have hurt him. I don't know where it came from, but one thing I've lived by is the commandment to "honor thy mother and father."

When I met him, I was a very soft spoken child. He often said, "Speak up, boy. I can't hear you. Speak up like a man." My mouth got bigger and I learned to speak up. That has served me well all of my life.

My sister Kathleen, the oldest, was a beautiful young woman with long dark hair. She had been removed from home by court order when she was nine and was returned in 1957 when she was fifteen. She had been in four different foster homes. She said that when anything was missing, she was blamed. She was lucky in the fact that she did not live far from one of our aunts where she would often go to get a decent meal and some love. When she came home, our mother had been hospitalized. She became a substitute mother to us boys and pretty much kept the house—which she ran reluctantly with a hardened disposition. She didn't have girlfriends or time to herself and was forced to take on adult responsibilities.

She also worked at my father's shop spray painting the lead figurines and packaging them for shipment. Then she started having children; it seemed like she was pregnant almost all the time, giving birth to a total of five children. Later in life, whenever I thought of having kids, I recalled her situation, the screaming children and diapers, and then I would think better of it. Kathy wasn't the brightest light bulb in the box. I remember her first car. She thought it needed only gas so one day the motor seized up. When asked if she had put oil in it, she asked, "What is oil?" The only education I got from my father about "the birds and the bees" was, "Practice like hell, son, but don't ever get it perfect. It seems like funny advice to have come from a man with seven children. This advice would have been better served if he had given it to Kathy because she practiced a lot and unfortunately got it wrong.

In the summer of 1961, we moved to a house on Depot Street. Because our family had grown due to all of us coming home, my father's boss purchased a larger house for us.

Kathy and her children lived on the first floor and "us men" lived on the second and third floors. Our television was a black-and-white-set with tubes. When the TV did not work, we would pull out every tube and go to the pharmacy next door. There was a television tube tester where we would test between fifteen and twenty tubes to find out which one was bad. We would scavenge the needed tube from another set that was sitting around the house and put the good television back together. When a television set was no longer functioning, my father took out the components and replaced them with a fish bowl. We wound up with four television cabinets, three of which had become fish tanks.

The other part of this is that on the roof was an antenna. It was a Channel Master Antenna. The house had a sheet-metal roof. Periodically we would have to go out on the lower porch roof and climb the ladder to the higher roof. One brother would pass the other brother a chair. He would crawl up to the center pitch of the roof, put the chair squarely on the ridge of the roof, climb up, and turn the antenna until he got the word that the reception was good. The "word" was hollered up from my father sitting in the living room with the television to one of us on the lower porch roof and relayed to whoever was on the upper roof. This ballet occurred several times a year.

In the middle of town was a general store with a soda fountain. The owner's name was Seymour Cohen. I remember one time when I had taken back some of my father's beer bottles for the deposit. I had a few pennies and I was dying for an ice cream, so I went and sat at the counter—a big man, all of twelve years old, my feet dangling off the stool. After he gave me the strawberry ice cream, which I have always loved, he asked me if I wanted some sprinkles. At the time, all he had were the little dark sprinkles. I asked if it would cost more, but he assured me it wouldn't. I eagerly devoured the cone. As I was eating it, he said, "Do you know what those sprinkles are?" I said, "No," with great anticipation of hearing what they were. He told me they were chocolate-covered ants. I must tell you that for many, many more years, I believed that the sprinkles on ice cream were chocolate covered ants.

About one hundred feet across the back yard was a two story garage with a sliding side door. Every morning my father would sit at the kitchen window and have his coffee before going off to work. Over time he could see that the door was becoming cracked and splintered and wondered what was causing it to happen. One morning he was a little late leaving for work. As he sat looking out the window, he saw arrows striking the door. He came right up stairs and made short work of our bows and arrows.

Another day, my father, complained that the garage was an eyesore and he wished that it were removed. He didn't ask me to take it down. I just took it upon myself. Working nights after school and weekends, I began disassembling it, board by board. I had to climb up and remove nails and drift pins to disassemble the post-and-beam barn and roof. I worked on it for maybe four weeks. As I took it down piece by piece with no equipment other than a hammer and rope, I stacked the materials in piles thinking that maybe somebody would buy the lumber. It was good lumber. The only thing that had deteriorated was the wooden floor.

I had taken about eighty percent of it down when one Saturday afternoon I noticed two cases of beer on the front porch. It was not like my father to flaunt his drinking. I asked about this and was told not to worry about it. Around noon, two fire trucks showed up. Men proceeded to pour kerosene over everything that remained of the garage, and also the neatly stacked pieces that I had removed.

He'd totally disregarded all the work I had done. He never said a word about it. He just had the guys come over and burn it all. Then they sat around drinking beer. I felt humiliated. That's how my father was. He never paid a compliment or shared his thoughts.

I had busted my butt, and he turned around and torched my efforts. I never trusted him after that.

My father was a member of the Pine Bush Fire Department. One day my brother John and I decided to run away from home. Being poor, we sneaked some hot dogs from the refrigerator and proceeded out of town. After what seemed like countless hours of walking—which in reality was about twenty minutes at most, we went underneath a long wooden bridge which went over a creek. We decided to cook our hot dogs there and started a camp fire. We heard fire sirens, but giving it no thought, we continued to roast our hot dogs. Soon the sirens became very loud and we heard voices. Looking up, we saw firemen coming toward us from both sides under the bridge. It soon became apparent that our camp fire smoke was mistaken for the bridge being on fire. Consequently, the firemen, including my father, proceeded to turn on the hoses extinguishing the fire and washing John and me into the stream bed below. This quickly ended my desire to run away from home. It also curtailed any desire I might have to cook.

We were often sent to Charlie Tressarrie's grocery store and would buy whatever we were instructed to get by my father or Kathleen. We did not have money for groceries each day. Charlie would write up our order on the side of a brown paper bag, total the items, and record the amount in his book. When my father got paid on Friday, he would settle up the account at the grocery store. Generally, we would get five Tobin's First Prize hot dogs, spaghetti, tomato paste, whole tomatoes, apple sauce, onions, five pounds of potatoes, bologna, cheese, butter, bread, milk, and Maxwell House coffee. This was our standard weekly shopping list. Bologna sandwiches now and then. Maybe once a month we would get an ice cream. We were not supposed to get candy, but once in awhile Charlie would slip candy in with the groceries. One of our main staples was potato pancakes. I can not tell you how many times we skinned our knuckles on the potato grater.

Having seen my father struggle to pay the grocer weekly, it became hallmark of my character as I got older that I pay my bills on time; I would go without rather than owe anyone. It also created a fear of poverty that is deeply ingrained in me.

There were two times a year that we would see Dad smile. One was Thanksgiving Day. There would be a massive feast with foods that we did not see for an entire year: turkey, red potatoes, and vegetables—a cornucopia of food. My sister, brothers, and I would all sit at the table, at the same time, and gorge ourselves with this feast. The second time was Christmas Eve. The Christmas tree was always put up then. My father was the choreographer. It had to be put together in a strict order. First, the string of large bulb lights (often referred to as outside lights) went on. Very careful attention was paid to the order of the colored bulbs so that the color pattern would repeat. Next, the aluminum stars were screwed in beneath the bulbs. Then came the placement of ornaments which also went in a precise pattern. Tinsel was put on one strand at a time. To cap this dazzling array was angel hair which, when put on right, was like a beautiful spider web. The Christmas tree was one thing, besides alcohol and cigarettes, which was never skimped on. These two days of the year were the times that we were all together, father and children functioning as a family.

One morning when I should have been in school, I walked past the small home town Gulf gas station, and my smart mouth got me into trouble. Mr. Don Hyde, the owner of the gas station, asked me how come I was not in school. I told him to go screw himself. (Actually, I used slightly more descriptive words.) Suddenly, his massive hand reached out and grabbed me. I feared an ass whooping, but he proceeded instead to hang me up on the rack that held fan belts and radiator hoses around the wall near the ceiling of the garage. After about ten minutes of me spewing vulgarities, he asked me, "Are you done yet?" When I finally shut my mouth, he lifted me off the rack and told me that if I went to school and cleaned up my mouth, he would not tell my father and I would be allowed to come and hang out around the garage. He was the first person ever to reach out and give me a sense of direction and purpose. He became my mentor and taught me respect and manners as well.

Mr. Hyde gave me a Chrysler Hemi engine. He told me that the way to find out how an engine works is to take it completely apart. My father said, "I don't want that damn thing in the house." So unbeknownst to my father, my brother John and I lowered a rope out the third floor window and hoisted the engine up through the window of the third floor and into our bedroom where, over time, I completely disassembled the engine. Having a dresser but not having many clothes to put in it, I began putting the crank, valves, cam, and other engine parts in my dresser. My father discovered my secret because I could not find a place to hide the bare engine block. Outraged that I had disregarded his instructions about bringing it into the house, he opened the window and proceeded to shove the engine block out the open window. It crashed through a wooden plank basement door and was soon followed by the remaining engine parts that were in my dresser. John and I had to immediately clean up the scattered engine parts and rebuild the basement door. I never did get that engine back together.

Another time, Mr. Hyde presented me with an old '57 Chevy and towed it over behind my father's house. The Chevy was a teaching tool. Mr. Hyde guided me through completely stripping the engine down to the bare block and rebuilding it, eventually getting it to run. I learned that it is better to do a job right than to do it poorly because a poor job will haunt you forever. He taught me to look at a job, to plan my work, to use tools, and to execute the plan. He insisted that I clean up my tools and put them back where they belonged. He told me that my tools are what put "bread and butter" on the table. This was a very valuable lesson which I applied all my life. I learned to respect other people, my tools, equipment, and myself. Most important, he taught me that no job was too small or large—to always do my best. He brought me to lunch or dinner at his home and included me over several years as a steady guest. His daughters and I would play basketball and I would work with him around his house. Don Hyde and his wife were my first introduction to what a family should be.

Before allowing the car to be towed to the back yard, my father had insisted and was assured that this would not wind up in the house. I should have given him assurance that no part of the house would become part of the car. I got the car to run about two years later. The problem was that it did not have an exhaust system. Being somewhat ingenious and devilish, I happened to notice the gutter down spouts that came from the second floor porch to the ground at my father's house (where, by the way, we were renters). I made quick work of removing these down spouts. With the use of a hack saw and bailing wire they became the exhaust system for my car. After the car was running and the glorious exhaust system was installed, I proceeded to take a cruise down our main street and back. I was sixteen and without a driver's license. There were no doors on the car and a milk carton served as a seat. My ego and self-adulation were only tempered by my father's great disapproval of the use of the gutter spouts for my exhaust. (He was one mad son-of-a-bitch.) I did not care. I got it to run once and that was its last run. Mr. Hyde was there for this maiden run and made me feel about sixteen-feet tall. I wanted to be loved and to be needed. I found that I was good at repairing things, using my hands and mind, and I was of use to people. When I had an opportunity to learn anything—I went for it, and so I eventually became a plumber.

My brother Arthur was home on leave from Basic Training in the Army when I first came home in 1961. On his second leave, he married Dorothy. He and his wife moved in directly across from my father's place of employment where they began their family: a son, Arthur Jack Knauer III and a daughter named Christina.

At that wedding, on December 22, 1962, I met my sister Rosemary for the first time. She was sixteen years old. In fact, that wedding was the first and only time that all of my father's children were at the same place at the same time. It was also the only time that all of his brothers and sisters and their spouses were with us. For just five minutes everyone was together for picture taking on the front porch. After that, at the wedding and reception, his brothers and sisters and their spouses were on one side of the room, and we children were on the other. For the first and only time I saw my father dressed up in a suit and dress shirt. This was a singularly proud moment for him.

On a very hot and humid day in July when I was thirteen years old, for some unknown reason, I went to the basement of our home. The buildings at Wiltwyck School did not have basements, and I had never been in one before. I went to investigate and found it dark, mysterious, and cool. I saw a large box mounted on the side of the furnace, and curiosity got the better of me. "What does it do?" I wondered. So I took it apart and discovered a wheel and float designed to control the flow of water. Everything was dried up and the wheel would not turn. When I could not get the motor to turn the wheel, I opened the electrical box, licked the tips of my fingers, and pinched the wire until I received a shock telling me I had the power wire. After I got the water running and the wheel to turn, I felt like I was six feet tall. What I had fixed was a humidifier. The humidifier is there only to run when the furnace is running and hot. I was very proud of myself even though I did not know what I had fixed. That was until later that afternoon when I went upstairs. Then—oh, my God—it was raining inside the house. I had fixed the humidifier all too well. The wallpaper was peeling and water was dripping from the ceiling. To say my father was not pleased is an understatement. He left a permanent impression on me in a place where the sun doesn't shine. That was the beginning of my life-long love affair with the plumbing and heating field.

In October of 1965, John was in the Army scheduled to be deployed to Viet Nam. Not wanting to take the chance that he would not return and that he would miss Christmas, I decided to put up a Christmas tree in the living room for an early Christmas. My father every morning would sit by the kitchen window and have his cup of Maxwell House coffee and a cigarette in the company of his parakeets before leaving for work. When I decided to have a Christmas tree early for John, the problem was where to find a tree.

Well, ladies and gentlemen, you got it. Charlie and I went over to my father's house. Out in the back yard, were two sixty-foot blue spruce pines. I climbed up one of the sixty-foot spruces and cut eight feet off the top. That night when my father came home, he was absolutely delighted to see the beautiful tree. That was until the next morning when he had his coffee and cigarette and looking out the window, saw the top of his prized blue spruce gone. The consequences were painful!

That same weekend, my best friend Charlie stopped by the house with his older brother's brand-new powder-blue El Camino equipped with a four-on-the floor 327 and a four-barrel carburetor. My brother John asked Charlie if he could take it for a drive. Charlie didn't know that John had no idea what he was doing. Within a mile of the house, he crashed it into a group of trees and totally wrecked it. Fifty-some years later, his brother still does not know that it was my brother John who was driving. Charlie took the blame.

Sometimes, after school or during the summer, I worked in my father's foundry. I helped move one-hundred-pound bars of lead, also known as "pigs," and stack them in piles. When the bars were melted, the lead was poured into steel molds. The molds were broken apart to remove the castings. We used to have to take a file and smooth down the excess ridge that was left after the molds were removed. The lead figures, after being buffed, were painted and boxed.

One time as my father was soldering in the air holes that were left after opening the molds, I sat across the room next to my father's friend Herman. We were filing the excess slag on the figurines. The triangular blades of the files were twelve inches long and ground to a razor sharp edge. The wooden handles were round and smooth.

Out of the corner of my eye, I saw Herman's file roll off the work bench and instinctively grabbed it. I scooped it up without thinking and accidentally rammed it into my thigh. It pierced the inside of my left thigh and came out the other side. Dad had instilled in us that it was a sign of weakness to show emotions. Thus in a quiet, almost sheepish voice, I called to my father, "Oh Pop." He hated to be called "Pop" because he was "no damn can of soda." The third time I called, he turned and saw the file protruding through my leg. He finished what he was doing, put his cigarette down, and came over to me. He cut the leg of my trousers and used his belt as a tourniquet on my leg. He called my sister from the other room and had her bring me to the doctor's office. The doctor was smoking a cigar when we got there. Without removing the cigar from his mouth, he grabbed a hold of the file and yanked it out. I was bandaged and sent home, no tetanus shot. Luckily, no major damage was done.

Another job at the foundry was sorting rocks. Barrels of rocks were shipped up from New York City. The rocks, native to New York State, were an assortment of fool's gold, granite, lime stone, etc. We would glue the rocks to name cards, placing an assortment of twelve rocks on squares in a cardboard box approximately six by twelve inches, and they would go to the Museum of Natural History in New York City.

The shop would receive half-inch-wide brass strips about one-foot long. We were allowed to take them home to make hot plates. At night, we would join the strips by pounding rivets into them. Each hot plate took about a dozen strips. The product was later sold in the city. This gave us a few cents for ourselves.

In the fall of 1961, at the age of twelve, I was enrolled in the

Pine Bush Elementary School. I had come from Wiltwyck School for Boys where I learned only the basic "ABC's" and math, so when I started school in Pine Bush, I was way behind. They started me in the fifth-grade along with another young man named Charles Edward Hancock. He was a baby-faced, red-headed boy. He was behind also, and we were both much older than the other boys. Soon we were inseparable outcasts—striking up what has become a life long friendship.

Charlie and I were always in the back of the classroom. When we did participate in the class, the other students snickered and laughed. The teacher ignored us. We became wise-asses and earned reputations as "tough guys." One day, Mrs. Callan said, "I hope that you are not as dumb as your parents." I hauled off and hit her. As I walked out into the hall, a male teacher who had seen me hit Mrs. Callan belted me.

We both were non-participants in school athletics. The thought of putting on gym shorts and going out in cold weather or playing football was not appealing. One day while gathering outside the boys' locker room, Coach Warneke put his key into the lock and went inside to chase everyone out. While he was inside, Charlie egged me on to lock him in. No sooner was my hand on the key, than the coach's big hand caught me upside my head, rolling me down the hall. Another fine mess you got me into, Charlie.

Because of our reluctance to go to school, Charlie and I were always the last ones to class. Almost every day, the teacher would rap our fingers with the edge of the ruler for being late. One day, frustrated by our tardiness and what I think was an attempt to humiliate us, Mrs. Callan asked, "Why are you boys always the last two to class?" Without skipping a beat, Charlie said, "If you had twenty girl friends with four sets of tits a piece and you had to pull them every day, you would be late too." The class erupted in laughter, as most of them lived on a farm and understood his reference to milking cows. We were immediately sent out to the hall to sand the old wooden, inkwell-type, desks where students had etched the names of girlfriends or boyfriends. I think Charlie and I have sanded every desk in the school at least twice.

Within the first week of attending school, Jimmy Dickerson began to tease me because it seemed like I wore the same clothes all the time. He continued to torment me until one day when we were taken out to the athletic field, he got in my face and I hauled off and hit him as hard as I could. He dropped like a sack of potatoes. The side of his neck swelled up. I was terrified that I had killed him. The coach told Charlie and me to get out of there. Luckily, there was no long-lasting injury, and I was never harassed again at that school. From then on, I'd walk away from a fight in fear of hurting someone. This was all before I knew about the coach's rules for handling conflicts

The coach was not only the "coach" but also the town justice. If there was any fighting, he had a simple remedy for resolving the dispute. He would take a piece of chalk and make a circle outside the gym. The boys would "go at it." When the first one was knocked down or out of the circle, the fight was over. They would shake hands and pray that the coach didn't hear of any further violence between them. He was the total arbitrator of our disagreements. We feared him more than each other.

The walk from my house to Charlie's was approximately two miles. One time on the way home, we got into a fight. His solution was to sit on me until I ran out of steam. I was so thin that Charlie would say if I turned sideways I would look like a zipper (because my nose stuck out.) And because I had very curly hair, he would often call me "Brillo head." He will tell you that I would fight at the drop of a hat no matter how big the other kids were. Having lived in a boy's school, I learned to fight or get whooped.

Charlie's folks lived on a small farm just outside of town. Mom Hancock always had an extra chair for anyone that came to her kitchen and would make do with whatever was on the stove—a bottomless pot. After many overnight stays, I was included by the Hancock family into their life. One day, after about a year of this, when I asked my father if I could go out to Charlie's house, he told me, "I don't give a shit, but if that suitcase goes out that door, it goes only one way." The ironic part of his statement was that we did not own a suitcase and everything I owned fit in a paper bag. With my father's blessing, I was "adopted." I have been part of their family for the past fifty-some years.

Charlie's father, a man I came to love as my own, was a steward on the passenger ship Queen Elizabeth II. I remember the first time Charlie's Dad came home and there I was down stairs in the bed room. That morning, nothing was said—as if I had been there all my life. When he wanted us to work, his favorite line was, "Give me five minutes boys, just five minutes." The five minutes often turned into hours. Many times he asked us to move rocks from the fields to a small stream to dam it up. Charlie and I moved every rock on that farm, at least twice. If only we had known that in later years people would be selling rocks as "Pet Rocks" and using rocks for massages; we could have sold a ton of rocks—who knew!

Before meeting Charlie, I did not know what cows, sheep, or even hogs were. I learned how to milk cows, feed and butcher hogs, and tend to the other animals. In the barn yard, there was a tractor shed with a sloping roof. Charlie would run and jump off the roof onto a pile of manure. Charlie wore boots and I just wore street shoes. When he called for me to jump. I remember saying, "What the hell?! Am I going to jump onto a pile of shit? I think NOT!"

One day, Charlie and I found a wooden row boat submerged in a neighbor's stream. It had a hole in its bow and the farmer said we could have the boat if we could get it out. After dragging the boat home, we figured we'd set sail on our pond. We nailed pie tins to the inside and outside of the bow and sealed our illustrious patch with tar. With repairs completed, we dragged it about a quarter of a mile to our pond.

On the day of our maiden voyage, I was wearing my first pair of new boots. They cost me $12.00. I felt like a king. Charlie's younger sister Nancy wanted to come with us, but we boys did not want a girl on our cruise. She ran across the field and launched herself from terra firma right through the bottom of the boat quickly sinking our efforts. Nancy cried that she was drowning. Charlie refused to rescue Nancy knowing that she could not drown in three feet of water. I went into the water and pulled her free. My boots got soaking wet, and when they later began to dry, they swelled, curled right up, and split apart. So much for rescuing damsels in distress.

Charlie and I were Boy Scouts for two days. We heard that the Scouts were going to go on a camping trip, so we asked if we could join. We went to one meeting on a Friday night. The overnight camping trip was scheduled for the next day. Saturday morning, in the dead of winter, we took a bus up to the Shawangunk Mountains. We spent the whole day making a lean-to out of pine tree limbs. We put our sleeping bags on a bed of pine needles. At night we had a camp fire with marshmallows and stories. At ten o'clock we went to bed. We pre-teens were on one side of the creek and the teenagers were on the other side with the counselors. That was until the older boys came over to our side, knocked down our lean-to, and filled our sleeping bags with snow. When the raiding party was over, Charlie and I told the counselors, "We quit; we want to go home." For the remainder of the night, we froze our asses off on the damp bedding. Bright and early Sunday morning we were taken home. Charlie and I made a new record for lasting in the Boy Scouts—two days.

Once before, Charlie and I had planned to camp out overnight. It was about a half-mile from home, and we could see the house lights. We spent the day digging fox holes. We made a camp fire and cooked marshmallows. Soon it got dark, and around ten p.m. Charlie got up and said, "Hell with this," and walked back to the house to sleep. I stayed the night.

When Charlie married, he and his family became avid campers. I, on the other hand, ask, "Where is the hotel room and hot showers?" He built their home where our camp site was. To get to Charlie's house, you must go over a small bridge that covers a stream. The stream is a result of all the rocks we picked up as kids building the dam.

Charlie worked for a farmer, Ira DuBois. On Saturdays, Ira was an independent transporter of livestock, delivering them between local farms and auctions. Ira was also a great tobacco chewer. There was always some type of spit container in his truck. Charlie often rode with him. Since Ira was Charlie's hero, he emulated him and took up tobacco chewing. One day Charlie was chewing tobacco while milking cows. He bet me five dollars I would not try it. Being

Mr. Big Shot, I took a mouth full and chewed. Charlie slapped me on my back and asked, "Well, how was it?" For all of you that don't know, you don't drink or swallow the juice. Damn, it will burn your insides out. I swallowed the juice. O my God, I thought I was going to die. I pushed that old cow out of the way and drank from the cow's watering trough. After drinking from the trough, I got a pitch fork and chased Charlie around the barn and barn yard for a half hour. If I had caught him, I would have stuck him. By the way, I never got my five dollars.

On Sundays, we went to church where Mom Hancock played the piano. Dad would stand in the pews and bellow out the words to the music. He was never embarrassed to sing, even though he could not carry a tune. They taught me respect for the Lord. One Sunday morning, while waiting to go to church, we boys, Charlie, his brother Bob, and I, were out in the field playing around with the old Model A truck. We would start it at the top of the hill, pop the clutch, ride it down through the barnyard and eventually out to the fields. This particular Sunday, as we entered the barnyard, the carburetor was leaking gas and the engine caught fire. The gas tank in a Model A is between the engine and the dash board. We quickly extinguished the fire, dirtying our white tee shirts with gas and soot. When we returned to the house, Mom was mad as the devil. She put us right into the car and proceeded to drag us to church. She marched us up to the front row of the church. We sat there with smelly tee shirts and soot on our faces.

We used to love coming home after church. We would play volley ball, eat, and go back to playing volley ball some more— Bonnie, Sonny, Bob, Charlie, Nancy, myself, and other friends. There was a true sense of family, probably the only family I will ever know. Charlie and his kids still continue to carry on with the tradition of volleyball.

Charlie and I were both sixteen-going-on-seventeen when, on December 9, 1965, we were called into the guidance office. The guidance counselor and our teacher talked about our leaving school. They were beating around the bush, trying to be delicate. We didn't get it. Finally, they flat out told us to leave school that day and never come back. They did not have to ask twice. We weren't sad to leave. It was time to go to work and make a living.

One of the constant drum beats of our teacher, Mrs. Callan, had been, "You boys are going to be nothing more than ditch diggers." She believed that without a high school education that is all that we would be good for. She was right. Charlie and I became expert ditch diggers. We installed countless water and sewer lines in mobile home parks, and public and private municipal water and sewer systems. this required math skills, reading and comprehending blue prints, and understanding manufacturer's technical manuals. I got "on the job training." I took courses in appliance repair and attended manufacturers' product demonstrations. I had to learn mathematics in order to comprehend such things as elevation, pitch, water flow analysis, and sewage flow. And, damn, being a "ditch digger" provided me with a good standard of living.

As the years went on, so did I. I moved to the Albany, New York region in the mid-seventies. Meanwhile, my sister Kathleen lived on the first floor in my father's house with her brood until a kitchen fire did an enormous amount of damage and made the home uninhabitable. My sister and her family moved to an apartment. My father took up residence in the shop where he worked. As long as he had his beer, his privacy, and his work, he existed. He had no spirit left.

On December 24, 1977, after visiting with Charlie in Pine Bush, New York, I drove around the corner onto Main Street. There was my brother Robert sprawled along the sidewalk, drunk as hell. I got out, got him into the truck, and drove over to my father's shop. It was a Saturday morning, and there was my father, all alone in the factory where he worked and lived, wearing his famous swordfish shirt and khaki pants. In his hand was a Camel cigarette. I helped Robert out of the truck and watched as he made his way into the building. He stumbled up the stairs to the small apartment he shared with my father. I saw my father standing up close to the huge windows—locked in a building that he was living and working in. I did not know if I should feel pity, shame, or embarrassment. It was late and I had about a two-hour ride to get home. I knew if I went in, he wouldn't have anything to say. So I gave my father a wave and proceeded back to Albany. I was at a point in life where I had my own car, a job, and friends. He had no outside socialization other than his time at Herman's Bar and Grill. I sensed a look of despair and disgust as he watched Robert stumble into the building. Perhaps watching his son so often in this condition broke his spirit. That was the last time I saw my father alive.

On December 29, I got a call from my sister Kathleen's husband that my father was dead. There had been a fire at the store where he worked and lived. The store front was directly across the street from the fire house. In an instant, the fire blew out of control, destroying the building which was one hundred years old, a block long, filled with cardboard, and supplied by several large propane tanks. It was a blessing that the fire happened when it did. If it had happened about thirty minutes later, there would have been about ten more people in the shop. My father was found sitting in his office where he and his dog were burnt alive. I believe that he sat on his couch making no effort to escape the fire. He waited to die. His life had been so devastated by events that death was a welcome relief. That damn dog loved him—would not leave him. I asked my father once what his dog's name was and he told me "Dog." My father being a consistent person always named his dogs "Dog" and this was his second "Dog".

I wonder if, as my father sat in his office waiting for the fire to consume him and the building burned around him, he welcomed death. I often thought about the demons that my father had to live with after the loss of my mother: the death of my sister, the destruction of his family, the loss of his home to a fire, and Robert's and John's irrational behaviors. I chose to take on some of those demons, but they were a blessing to me.

That was my "Pop." He was laid to rest on New Year's Day.

4. A Working Life

I've never been a stranger to work. From first days that I became friends with Charlie, we worked on his farm and at other area farms taking care of dairy animals and hogs as well as other chores. We mowed lawns and shoveled snow. Whatever jobs we could find that would pay, we took, and we played as hard as we worked.

About the age of eighteen, I learned a valuable lesson. There was an explosion at a chemical plant outside of Middletown, New York. The owners of the plant put a notice in the newspaper seeking workers to clean up the site. They offered $5.75 an hour for what was strictly "bull work." When I arrived, there was a large crowd of men applying for the job. I met with the foreman and offered to work for a dollar less an hour, figuring I would then get the position in spite of my age and inexperience. Up to that point, he seemed amenable to my working for him. Hearing my asking price, he said, "Sorry, I can't use you." Upon leaving, I turned and asked why he did not want me. He told me, "If you don't think you are worth the $5.75 that I am paying everyone else, then I don't want you." After leaving the building and before getting in my truck, he came out and told me that I was hired if I would work for what he was paying. This was a perfect lesson which followed me the rest of my life. I learned how to bid on jobs, especially when I worked for myself. I worked that summer cleaning up the destroyed chemical plant.

Another time, Charlie and I worked unloading one hundred pound bags of animal feed from railroad box cars. We started early in the morning before the sun came up and the outside temperature was about sixty degrees. We started in the center and as we worked toward the back of the car, it rose to over one hundred degrees. I thought to myself that there had to be a better way of earning money. That's when Charlie and I changed from doing bull work to using our brains and hands as plumbers. Plumbing and heating did require a great deal of back breaking labor, but it was a job that we loved. Plumbing and heating became our life-long work.

Charlie and I went to work for B & C Oil Company and were mentored by two seasoned plumbers, "Dutch" and "Cupie." We learned plumbing, heating and pool playing.

Mother Hancock would often recite this poem:

A Scottish proverb:

"If wishes were horses, beggars would ride,
    If turnips were swords, I'd wear one by my side.
    If "ifs" and "ands" were pots and pans,
    There'd be no need for tinkers' hands."

I kept the first line in my head as a constant reminder that wishing gets you nothing but working does.

In the 1960's, the United States was at war in Vietnam and there was a draft. My father had served in the Calvary division and later as a mess sergeant in the Army during World War II. All of my uncles had served as well. It was just expected that we boys would follow in their footsteps. Arthur, John and I all volunteered to join the Army. The underlying reason for joining up was to get away from the abject poverty and have instead new clothes, three meals a day, health care, and a chance to "see the world." The Army was the place most high school dropouts went. Juvenile delinquents sent before judges were often given a choice of going into the Army or to jail. The Army was a refuge for a lot of young men looking for a better life. There were three types of people in the Army: the National Guard Reserves which were referred to as "weekend warriors," those that were drafted, and ones that joined voluntarily. I enlisted in April 1966.

John had joined and was scheduled to go to Vietnam in October. I assumed that I would also be going to Vietnam. The gathering point for the recruits from my region was Fort Hamilton in Brooklyn. During testing, I was asked, in a tone of ridicule, where would I like to be assigned. (Remember, I was a very skinny and scared young man—only eighteen years old.) Sheepishly, I said, "Paris would be nice." This resulted in an outburst of laughter from the fat, overweight recruiting sergeant who mocked me in front of the entire group.

Basic Training was at Fort Dix, NJ, after which we went to Fort Jackson in South Carolina. When we left from New York City, there was snow on the ground and upon our arrival in South Carolina it was very, very hot. We were greeted kindly by a staff sergeant of small stature. "Gentlemen," he said, "Would you please be kind enough to disembark from the train and get on the buses." We did so. It was exceedingly hot outside and, coming from the North, we were dressed for winter. Once on the buses, we proceeded to open the windows. The staff sergeant, in an incredibly loud, booming voice, yelled, "You are in the Army now. Close the fucking windows. Your soul belongs to God, but your ass belongs to me!"

After getting off the bus, we were made to stand in line. The sergeant ordered all of the men who had a college education to stand to one side and the high school graduates to stand in another group. To the rest of us he shouted, "All you fucking dummies stand here." I figured that not having an education meant that my group would have to do the heavy or demeaning work. As the guys who had gone to college smirked, the sergeant told them that they would have to do some digging. We "fucking dummies" were told to relax while the high school graduates were ordered to start shoveling sand. The college boys used wheel barrows to move the sand to another location. The lesson taught by the sergeant was that we were all equal.

One of the first places we were taken was to the barber shop where we became even "more equal." Many men in the Sixties had hair far longer than most women. One minute a guy had hair down his back and next minute he was bald. Every one of us looked the same.

I was assigned to the 97th Engineer Battalion and did my M.O.S. training (Military Occupational Specialty) as a stationary engineer taking care of building maintenance—basically plumbing and heating.

The drill sergeant, a Korean, would come into the barracks and drop a quarter on our beds. If it didn't bounce, he would rip the bedding off and throw it on the floor. Then we would have to remake the bed. There was an African-American soldier with poor personal hygiene whose bunk and foot locker were always a mess. The sergeant would tear into him and toss his bunk and foot locker. Then he would do the same to a few others whose equipment was in great shape. This happened several times. Finally he left a metal bucket and scrub brush on the barrack's floor. We got the message. We took that soldier into the shower and gave him a "GI shower" with the scrub brush. After that, his hygiene and belongings were always fit for inspection.

The sergeant was also against smoking after lights out. When he caught someone smoking, he would make him go outside and dig a hole six foot deep and six foot square and bury the cigarette butt.

This same drill sergeant had served in several theaters of combat. He would come out of his room after lights out, drunk and having a flash back of his days in combat. He would start punching lockers and screaming in Korean. "Let's get dressed. We're going for a walk," he'd command. This walk turned out to be a five mile run in the middle of the night with a full field pack which weighed about seventy-five pounds. We'd get back just in time to shave, dress, and turn out for inspection. We didn't dare complain to a senior officer.

We were in training during the time the army changed weapons. Because of all the time Charlie and I had spent target shooting and hunting, I easily qualified as an expert. Our first rifles were M1s—heavy World War II weapons. In 1966, the army issued us M16's, lightweight composite weapons, to test. We took them through real life conditions, testing them in mud, rain, and sand. On maneuvers we discovered that in a rapid fire position they would jam and not discharge the spent shell. The breech was made of steel, and a little bit of sand or rust would cause it to jam easily. It was also easily spotted when fired at night because of the white flash from its muzzle. The second batch came with a stainless steel breech and a flash suppresser. It was put into mass production and battle-tested in Vietnam. It is still the military weapon of choice today.

We assumed that we would all go to Vietnam, but about five of us were sent to the European theater because we had siblings already serving in Vietnam. We were sent to France in late 1966 and assigned to the 97th Engineers. We landed in Frankfurt, and I had several hours to wait for the train which would take me to the base in France. In front of the train station were five streets, like fingers. I walked down the streets and got the shock of a lifetime. The store fronts displayed the kind of sex offered in that brothel. There were naked women, women on women, women in leathers, women in bondage, and men with men. It was a cornucopia of sex, and all one had to do was pay the price and go in. I was eighteen and thought I had balls that dragged the ground. It turned out I was so frightened I could not get back to the train station fast enough. Nothing in my experience had prepared me for this.

More culture shock awaited me in France. Men wearing shorts were playing soccer in the snow. Farm animals were not in barns, but lived instead on the ground floors of the houses to help heat them.

General De Gaulle ordered US troops to vacate the country. My battalion was assigned to go throughout the countryside to former military installations, disassembling buildings and packing them up to be shipped to other countries for later use. What could not be reused was destroyed.

After France, we were transferred to Germany where we did

Base Maintenance repairs: plumbing, heating and construction. I had my first sexual exploit in Germany. I'd met an officer's wife while doing some maintenance work in the officer's quarters. Enlisted men were not allowed to fraternize with female officers or officers' wives. However, when she opened that door in that long red negligee, I got the education of a lifetime. We agreed to meet the coming weekend in Frankfort. I was able to get a week-end pass and met her there. After leaving her around midnight, I missed the last train and had to walk twenty miles back to base. No sooner had my head hit the pillows, than reveille sounded.

After two years, I returned to Fort Reilly, Kansas to await my discharge. At Fort Reilly, with less than thirty days left in the Army, we were called "short-timers." As "short-timers," we did not do guard duty or KP. We just coasted. I went to the base dentist while there. I'd never been to a dentist, and not only did I have a severe overbite, but also many of my teeth were rotten. During the cleaning, the dentist suggested correcting my overbite. That meant breaking the jawbone and realigning it. They did the surgery which required wiring my jaw closed for ten weeks. They pulled one tooth so that I could drink broth through a straw. It was an ordeal, but it has benefited me throughout my life.

When President Eisenhower died on March 29, 1969, we were assigned to securing the area around his tomb and putting his command car inside the museum. After the dignitaries left, we put the granite capstone on his grave. That was my final assignment.

On April 15, 1969 (or there about), a friend and I went in to town to celebrate our discharge. After some heavy drinking, we were just flat out drunk when we were returning to base. I remembered I had a fifth of Southern Comfort under the seat. Since we couldn't bring liquor onto the base, I proceeded to polish it off. For the next three days I thought I was dying. Then I found myself on a Greyhound Bus headed to New York with my discharge papers in my pocket. The only thing I left the Army with was the clothes that were on my back. I hadn't shaved or bathed for three days, trying to sober up. I smelled. I was the most disgusting human being on the planet. I sat in the back of the bus in the last seat all by myself on the way to New York. That's my memory of being discharged from the U.S. Army.

The army was as close to a functioning family as anything I had ever known. It gave me a format for life. I learned to work in a structured environment and to cooperate, as well as some of the social skills I'd need in the workplace. It taught me how to deal with life and its responsibilities.

After leaving the Army on September 3, 1969, I tried returning to Pine Bush School as a student. I was twenty-one by then. I drove a school bus trying to earn money, and then I went to class with my passengers in order to complete my education. I made it until February twenty-third when, once more, the guidance counselor asked me to leave because my grades were not making it. I think I was the only student in Pine Bush school history to be thrown out twice.

I needed to earn more than I was making at the time. I didn't consider seeking public assistance. My older sister, who had several children out of wedlock, was on public assistance. My brothers Robert and John were constantly on welfare and other social programs which gave them subsistence. Seeing them exist on the fringes of life motivated me to do better.

From April 1969 to June 1976, I worked in a succession of

plumbing and heating positions in the private and public sectors. I returned for awhile to B&C Fuel Oil Company and John Christ Plumbing and Heating where my love affair with plumbing and heating had begun. There I rejoined my life-long friend, Charlie Hancock. I later drove a fuel oil delivery truck.

During this time, I got my first apartment. Charlie and I decided to wallpaper the bathroom. We went over to my father's house and took left-over rolls of wallpaper and picked up a case of beer. We papered the bathroom at the same time that we consumed the beer. Nothing like two drunken men wallpapering! It looked just beautiful to us. It was a kaleidoscope of colors. That is, until the landlady saw it. The room soon was white once more. I was forced to remove the paper and paint it, at my cost, of course.

In 1971, I worked at Horton Hospital in Middletown, New York as an ambulance driver. Part of the driver's responsibility was to take the deceased from the wards to the morgue. As I entered the morgue for the first time, the coroner turned and handed me a human brain. He thought he would frighten me. That didn't bother me at all, but what scared the hell out of me was the first time I took a dead body to the morgue alone. It was in the middle of the night, and I pushed the gurney along a dark hallway lit with one forty-watt light bulb. I was halfway down the hall when the switch board operator cleared her throat to speak over the public address system. Before she could say a word, I let go of the gurney and ran. Oh yes, I was scared as hell then.

We drivers had to help the undertakers remove the corpses from the cooler and load them into the hearse. They would tip us for that service. The morgue was at the very back of the hospital in the sub level. One day during a heavy snow and ice storm, the undertaker,

Sandy De Witt, a man that later buried my father and my brothers Robert and John, was unable to get the hearse to the morgue level. The back of the hospital was like a horse shoe: the cardiac wing on one side, the maternity ward on the other, and a loading dock in the middle. It was hospital policy not to deliver the deceased from that dock because it wasn't sheltered from view. My supervisor, Mr. E. S. Smith, said to wait until dark and use that dock because of the snow and ice. The dock was covered in ice, and as I walked out, my feet slipped out from under me. My hands squeezed the release and collapsed the gurney. The body which was in a white plastic bag slid right off the gurney and into a large dumpster. Next, I was inside the dumpster up to my waist in garbage, wearing a white shirt and black slacks, hoisting the body over the edge while the undertaker, wearing a dark gray top coat with a black fur collar and a beautiful fedora, grappled with this run-away body to get it back on to the stretcher and into the hearse. Damn. If anyone had seen this circus, there would have been a mad rush for the exits.

There was a sign on the front of our ambulance which read "You call. We haul." One morning when we had an emergency call, we proceeded down the hill from the hospital with lights and sirens. The first car we came upon happened to be the hospital administrator's. He pulled over and allowed us to pass. When we returned to the hospital and were wheeling the patient in, the administrator was waiting there screaming like a crazy man, "Who put that sign on the ambulance?" We had no idea what he was yelling about. We walked out with him and there it was, "You kill'em—we chill'em." We found out later that one of the emergency room doctors had added this logo as a joke.

There was a small hospital just outside the city of Goshen that did not have an ambulance, so the local undertaker would use his hearse for transport. When there was an accident, I would show up in the ambulance and there would be the hearse answering the call as well. Many times people damn near had a heart attack thinking they were headed for the morgue. We would reassure them that they were being taken to the hospital and not to the morgue.

A coworker and I knew a candy-striper who kept asking if she could see the morgue. That was against the hospital policy, but, nonetheless, Robert laid on the gurney and I covered him with a sheet. I had arranged for the candy-striper to meet us at the freight elevator. With the candy-striper shaking and pale as a ghost we made our way down to the sub-basement and the long dark hallway to the morgue. Bob stayed as rigid and quiet as possible until I tapped him on his shoulder. From under the sheet a deep, heavy voice said, "Morgue, please." With that, our candy-striper screamed and passed out cold. Robert slid out from under the sheet, and we picked her up and placed her on the gurney. Yes, Ladies and Gentleman, we slid her into the morgue's empty cooler. When she came to, you could hear her screaming throughout the hospital. Both Robert and I received three days off without pay.

There was a delicious side benefit while working at Horton Hospital, a smorgasbord of single or divorced women. Every night, I would meet someone different at eleven and go out on a date. I would often wait at the time clock for my latest date. The security guard, Julius, would razz me, calling me "Killer," as it seemed that I never dated the same girl twice.

One of these dates was a fiery red haired woman named Patricia Eurich. We were going to go out for a couple of drinks and play some pool, but we never made it inside the bar. We got to talking in my truck, and I realized that Patricia was different from my other dates—not someone to be chased around the pillow. I admired how she handled herself and spoke. I thought of my best friend Charlie, and the next day I introduced her to him, also a red head. They now have been married for almost forty years. Introducing them is one of the best things I've done in my life.

At the same time that I was working for the hospital from 11:00 pm to 7:00 am, I worked during the day from 8:00 a.m. to 4:30 p.m. for Sears doing service and installation. This is what allowed me to buy my first home by the age of twenty-two.

Sears, at the time, bought their vans with only a driver's seat. One day a supervisor was assigned to spend the day in the van with me. He had to sit on a milk crate. While we were going through a quiet neighborhood, a large German shepherd began to chase the van trying to bite the tire. Forgetting that the supervisor was in the van, I bellowed out, "Come forth, O mighty dragon, so I might smite thee with my sword." In the following four years working for Sears I never had another supervised ride.

While at Sears, I attended many four-week classes on appliance repairs, refrigeration, and heating and cooling units. I took the opportunity whenever any educational classes were offered. Later in life I was able to use what I learned in my plumbing and heating career.

I took the New York State's Stationary Engineer Exam and received a grade in the 90's. Stationary Engineers run power plants for generating hot water or steam to produce heat and electricity. I quit working at Sears and Horton Hospital in 1972 and started to work at Walden Auto Parts. I worked behind the counter as a salesman.

In the winter of 1975, I was driving to work in a blinding snow storm. I missed a turn and soon my truck was flying over a cliff into the Walkill River. The engine revved loudly and all I could think was, "Oh shit!" The truck slammed though the ice and began sinking. I tried opening the door and could not because of the ice and water against the door. I rolled down the window and swam to shore. At the time, I had a full beard. Almost at once, every part of me froze. I tried hitchhiking, but no one stopped to pick up a human Popsicle.

During July 1976 when I worked for RAL Plumbing and Heating, a wholesale plumbing distributor, in Middletown New York, I had to deliver a load of cast-iron tubs. Cast-iron tubs are very heavy, about three hundred or more pounds. It was Friday and my boss said that after making my deliveries I could quit and head home. I delivered the twelve tubs and was heading back to the warehouse. Hot, tired, not paying attention, and driving just a little too fast on a winding road, I did not see the warning lights flashing at the train tracks. I heard the train whistle, saw only the massive head light, braked, and skidded on loose gravel colliding into the side of the lead engine of a freight train. I bounced off the front engine, and bounced three or more times into the box cars. The whole front end of the truck was sheared off and the frame of the two-ton flatbed truck was badly twisted. The Village of Chester Police and State Police arrived on the scene; they had all they could do to peel my fingers from the steering wheel. I walked away without a scratch. The Chester Police officer asked the engineer, "Wasn't there a way that the train could have avoided hitting the truck?"

I was issued two tickets. One was for not having an insurance card. It had been kept in the glove compartment, the contents of which were now scattered up and down the tracks. The second ticket was for failure to yield at the railroad crossing. I went home and polished off a bottle of Jim Beam. The magnitude of the accident did not sink in until several hours later.

After RAL Plumbing and Heating, I began work at the state-run Middletown Psychiatric Facility. It was a coal-burning operation. Outside of the building on an elevated track, rail road cars of coal were delivered. Often in the winter, we would find the coal frozen solid. We would have to climb up the side of the open box car and use six foot long steel bars to break up the frozen coal in order for it to be dumped from the bottom of the box cars. Doing this often caused what used to be referred to in Vaudeville as "Blackface." As the cars were emptied, we used a large front end loader to scoop up the coal, dumping it into a 20' x 20' hole in the ground. There it was crushed and carried through a series of conveyer belts to the coal bunkers at the top of the building. Beneath the coal bunkers there was a scale and a smaller bunker where we would load the coal and weigh it before putting it into the hopper of the boiler.

The coal dust and the heat of the coal fire boilers often made tedious work, and, for some levity, we would periodically have water balloon battles. The scale traveled along the ceiling from one end of the building to the other under the storage bunkers of coal. We rode with the scale along the track in order to weigh the coal before dumping it into the boiler hopper. This was a good vantage point from which to drop water balloons.

On weekends when the refrigeration plant was idle, we would climb up the ice discharge chute and use ice tongs to steal enormous blocks of ice. By putting a fan in front of the ice blocks, we created air conditioning to suppress the stifling heat of the boilers.

A coal fire plant uses wood to start the boiler. One day, someone fell asleep and let the hopper become empty, and the boiler went down. In order to restart the boiler, we needed wood badly. In desperation, we chopped up a desk and chair and tossed it into the boiler. We added about five gallons of gasoline, and the boiler was restarted.

Every morning, we went into the locker room and lined our lunch pails along the window ledge which was the coolest place in the building. At lunch time, we would notice that some of the contents were missing from our thermos bottles. First one of us, then another, would say, "I'm going to find the bastard that is stealing from my thermos." About a week later, as we all sat around having lunch, one man piped up and said, "I caught the son-of-a-bitch that has been stealing from our thermoses." We asked who and how. He said, "I pissed in my thermos this morning." The culprit immediately began throwing up. We all had a good laugh, and that ended the lunch box pilfering.

In 1976, I moved to Albany County. I had two interviews. One was for a position as a stationary engineer at Coxsackie Correctional Facility. As I arrived in Coxsackie, before going to the interview, I decided to see what Coxsackie had to offer. I was struck by how rundown "downtown" was and how few businesses existed. (It's ironic that many years later, I would make downtown Coxsackie my home and become mayor of my street.) When I went into the prison for my interview, I had to empty my pockets and show paper identification. I heard the heavy steel door close behind me and the foreboding sounds resonating from inside the prison: whistles, the slamming of steel on steel, and voices yelling. My reaction was, "Let me the hell out of here." I did not want to work there.

The other interview was in Albany at the Office of General Services. I was hired as a stationary engineer at the State University. Most industrial buildings operate under steam pressure. The university is unusual as it uses hot water throughout instead of steam. Depending on the time of day, the season, and the activities in the building, the heating load would fluctuate. When the load was heavy, we would chain the safety valve to maximize the output of the boilers. One day when the day crew arrived, we noticed steam coming from around the doors and windows. We discovered the stationary engineer and fireman sound asleep with their feet up on the table. There was about four inches of boiling hot water on the floor. If the sleeping men had stepped onto the floor, the hot water would have boiled the skin right off their feet. Luckily, we were able to wake them without having their feet touch the floor.

The biggest and dumbest klutz attack that I had while working in an industrial heating plant happened there. On the back of the boiler there was a fifty-five gallon barrel attached to what is called a "soot collector." There are valves between the fifty-five gallon barrel, the collection area, and the exhaust area. Every eight hours, the valve to the exhaust would be closed and the captured soot would be allowed to cool before being dumped into the fifty-five gallon barrel for disposal. One day I forgot to close the valve between the cooling chamber and the drum. As the hot ash fell into the drum, the entire boiler room and engineering room were covered with several inches of heavy black soot. The hot ash melted the drum and the ash scattered everywhere. It took us about a week of constant scrubbing, to get the rooms cleaned. I got razzed hard by my fellow workers for this mistake.

In the late 1970's, after working for New York State in several different divisions doing plumbing, heating, and service, I went on to work at Main Care Heating and Cooling for a year or two as a boiler and furnace installer. Here I met Arthur Van Apledoorn, the best sheet metal worker that I have ever met. He makes customized duct work for homes and small businesses.

One time, Arthur and I were working on the Bethlehem Town Hall extension. We were up on the roof getting ready to cut through and install a roof heating and cooling unit when we heard, "Watch out for the bump! Watch out for the bump!" Seconds later we heard, "Ma's going to kill you!" We looked over the edge of the roof and saw a boy on a bike and another boy scooping up the remains of a pizza.

Another time while working on the same roof, I was one floor down on a ladder inside the building, looking up through the hole we had cut through the roof. Artie was on the roof guiding the crane that was lowering the heating and cooling unit down to me. Just then, a brunette walked past the ladder that I was on. She had a body that could melt butter five hundred feet away and was wearing a revealing low cut dress. I turned to look at her and signaled Artie. He leaned over the hole in the ceiling to look. All of a sudden, he slipped through the opening, knocking me and the ladder over. As we fell, down came about forty feet of ceiling, tiles, and lights. Oh, my god, what a mess! The brunette smiled and continued walking on. These incidents were the beginning of a life-long friendship. Artie and I enjoyed working with each other for over thirty years.

I was getting tired of working for supervisors that did not know their asses from their elbows and did not know what field work was about. They often put men in positions that they were not suited for. Other times they would send us out to install a furnace at a location where the entrance was too small for the furnace. We would have to completely disassemble the furnace and reassemble it in the basement. Then our bosses would bitch about how long the job had taken. We told them if they had measured the job properly we would not have taken the additional time.

The final insult of working for others happened when I was working on Manning Boulevard in Albany, New York. I had put a new oil burner gun on an old furnace. I could not get fuel to the pump. With the new pump, the oil should have been sucked right up. I tried everything to get it working with no success. Then I called and told my boss that I thought there was a foot valve in the oil tank. My boss said, "You don't know what the hell you are talking about. They never put foot valves in oil tanks." I got so mad with his response that I was determined to solve this problem before I went home. It was after dark when I pulled my truck alongside the customer's house, focusing the head lights on where I wanted to work. I dug down five feet, disconnected and pulled the rods from the fuel tank. Sure enough, there was a foot valve on the end of the pipe that had rotted off, and that is why I couldn't get oil. After I replaced the foot valve and put down a new rod, the furnace started within five minutes. It then took a couple of hours to clean up the basement, put the tools away, and back fill the hole in the yard. Luckily, it was sandy loam and easy to rake.

The original job was fairly simple and should have taken about two hours, not from 5:00 in the afternoon until 11:00 at night. I was so goddamn mad that I went back to Main Care's office. I took the five foot stinger suction rod along with the rusted off, oil-soaked foot valve and laid it across my boss's desk. The next morning when my boss came in, he was furious and told me I was fired. I said,

"Oh no, don't you see that I'm cleaning out my locker. I quit, and you can shove the job where the sun don't shine." From this point on, I started to work for myself and have completely loved my work and customers.

In between regular jobs, during the summer of 1976 through the spring of 1981, I worked part-time establishing Knauer Plumbing and Heating. From 1981 until I went blind in 2002, I worked for myself.

While trying to start my own business, I sub-contracted my services to a company that installed commercial and light industrial dual-fuel boiler guns. These very complicated guns were manufactured by Peabody, Gordon, and Piatt. I installed one of these in a commercial greenhouse in Schenectady, New York, and it ran beautifully with no problems switching from natural gas to oil and back. Yet, the next morning the boiler was cold. When I hit the reset control, the boiler fired and ran all day. During the day, I monitored the gas pressure, the fuel oil pressure, and the electrical system of the burner. All that day, from eight in the morning to six at night, the burner fired each and every time with normal function. Still, on the following day, it was off in the morning. The customer complained that if by Friday the problem was not resolved, he wanted the burner removed. The burners run about $10,000.00. Being that I was a sub-contractor, if it didn't work, I would not get paid.

That evening I brought in my lawn chair, coffee, and sandwiches. With all my testing equipment attached to the boiler, I parked myself in front of the boiler. Two men from Niagara Mohawk Gas and Electric joined me. We monitored the electric power from the pole transformer directly to the burner through the entire electrical system of the building and the gas pressure from the road to the burner. The boiler fired with no problems during the evening. At midnight, the utility personnel left. At one o'clock and two o'clock everything was fine. Finally, about three in the morning, as I sat in my chair, I felt a drop of water hit my head. I looked up and saw that the entire roof of the greenhouse had condensation dripping from it. The glass infrared eye is a safety device, which shuts down the burner if there is no fire within fifteen seconds of start up. I thought that if there was condensation on the glass ceiling, there might be some on the glass eye. I unscrewed the fiber optic eye, and found there was a little bit of moisture on it. The glass, as well as the roof, had gotten condensation from the cool night air. I wiped the eye, and the burner fired without any problem. The eye was mounted to the gun with a three inch porcelain holder. I drilled a quarter inch hole in the holder that would allow the condensation from the eye to drip to the floor. It was a fifty cent fix on a $15,000.00 job.

One of the strangest service calls that I ever had while working for myself was when a customer called up and said she had a plugged sewer line. I arranged for a friend to bring a back hoe and we uncovered the septic tank. After pulling the cover off, we discovered hundreds of condoms floating just inside the intake of the septic tank. Condoms do not sink; they float. They created a dam which plugged up the sewer line. After breaking up the soap on the surface and scooping the condoms into a bucket, we back filled and raked over the tank. Just as we were ready to leave, she asked what we had found. Trying to be discrete, I told her, "You cannot flush condoms down the sewer." I showed her the pail of condoms. She asked if she could purchase the pail. Totally mystified, I said she could have it. As she picked up the pail and started walking toward the house, she turned, looked over her shoulder, and said, "He doesn't need them with me."

One winter day, the weatherman was calling for a major storm. I had an Artic Cat snowmobile parked on a trailer in my front yard. When it started to snow, I decided to go out, check the fuel level, and make sure it would start. I climbed onto the trailer, with one knee on the snow mobile and the other foot on the running board. As I touched the throttle, the machine shot off the trailer. To the right there was a twenty-five foot high oak tree, to the left there was a large tool storage shed, and in front of me was a wire fence used to surround a horse farm. Quickly, wanting to select the direction where I'd receive the least injury, I steered for the fence and smashed my right hand on one of the fence posts. The sled got tangled up in the wire fence. It was Friday night and it hurt like hell. I could bend my fingers but with a great deal of pain. All day Saturday, I worked changing a water tank and favoring my right hand the best that I could. By about 4:00 a.m. Sunday morning, the pain became overwhelming. I could not put the pain out of my mind as I could so many other times previously. I went to Memorial Hospital in Albany, New York where I had my hand x-rayed. After waiting about ten minutes, the x-ray technician put the film on the lighted viewer, and said, "It only hurts?" He showed me I had seven broken bones between the first three fingers. Before this I had never broken a bone in my body. A temporary cast was put on until Monday when Dr. Jabbur operated, putting pins in to hold my fingers while healing. Being self-employed, I still needed to go to work. In order to keep the cast dry, I purchased a loaf of bread, fed the bread to the birds, and used the bread cover to cover my cast.

Then I thought of getting married and creating what I was

missing in my life, a family. Then I took up drinking, and with more passion, irresponsibility, and disregard for the people around me, I just used women for one thing. Thinking I could build that family I never had, I went through a succession of failed marriages. I have been married five times. Sometimes it was outside influences that had a big effect on my marriages and when a love falls apart, it's better to simply walk away. To tell you how pitiful my desire to be loved and cared for was, when someone asked me many years later what my wives' names were, I could remember only three of the five.

When I married my first wife, I was working two jobs—the beginning of a life time of hiding in my work. At twenty two, I owned my first home. When she went elsewhere for love, our marriage fell apart. She came back and wanted to talk and try to work it out, and I chased her away. Once more my mouth, opened before engaging my brain, and with more bravado and less compassion and understanding, I chased her away. I was going to be damned if I'd ever let anyone get inside me ever again.

Grieving

George William Knauer

I grieved as we went through the divorce,
But yet shed not a tear.
I hid my shame and despair in plain sight,
So that no one would see it.
I screamed when the divorce was final,
But not a sound was heard.
My heart still screams silently how much I loved her.

Only when I am laid to rest
Will the memory of the love we once shared
Be finally put to rest.

My work became my "mistress" to which I devoted the rest of my life. That is not to say that I have never remarried. I remember being happy in the photos, but the only ones that I ever made happy were the divorce lawyers. I thought true love came with a license.

Gentlemen, if you ever wish to try to save your marriage don't drop a cast iron boiler on your wife, or by the end of the day it will be your ex-wife.

My work has been the one glue that has held my life together. The work was hard and the hours were long, but these were the best years of my life. I found something in plumbing that I loved. I never thought that I was working for "customers", but for "friends." I found my "family" in my town and in the people I worked for. They became much more than customers. I loved plumbing and doing work for people. I never thought of myself as a "businessman." It wasn't until my community started the Coxsackie Chamber of Commerce and asked me to join that I learned to consider myself a businessman.

When I came to Coxsackie, I rode through downtown. Most of the buildings were either vacant or in a wretched state of disrepair. After my last divorce, I was in a position to buy a three-story that I had worked in for many years. It was an old run-down tenement with the windows falling out, no central heat, old knob and tube wiring, lathe and plaster—just completely run down. The back yard was a swamp. When it rained, the water would flood the back yard and basement because the road was higher than the back of the building. I had worked in this building many times as a plumber, and I knew what the potential of the building and what the rest of the downtown could be.

I bought Twenty-One Reed Street in April of ninety-five. I loved this building. My original plan was to clean up, paint, and paper, but I began to work on the kitchen counter and the next thing I knew my hands had ripped it from the wall. Then the cabinets jumped out the window. People began to ask me what all the debris was in the back yard. I told them, "It jumped out the window and committed suicide—same thing with the bath-room fixtures." Before I knew it, the entire interior of the building was in the pile. So I was forced to completely renovate all three floors with new kitchens, baths, and floors. It turned out to be an extraordinary building. I had an outside porch put on the back of my building with an exquisite view over-looking the park and the Hudson River.

My form of relaxation since the age of twelve was photography. I really enjoyed capturing the beauty of the outdoors, and I had done some photos of public events. My biggest thrill was photographing Hillary Clinton when she came to our village on April 15, 2000 as the former first lady of the United States and Senate candidate. At the time, she was running for New York State Senate. I was asked by Mayor Henry Rauch to be the official photographer for her visit. I got about an hour and a half of unfettered access photographing her and was issued a temporary Secret Service badge so that I could be allowed to move around freely. On May 29, 2002, the year I went blind and had a mild stroke, she returned to Coxsackie as Senator. I was just beginning to walk. At the arrangement of the Mayor, she took time out of her busy schedule to meet with me and my sister. Her security agents were saying, "We do not have time," and in a clear, firm voice, she said, "I am making time." If she had not been on one side holding me and my sister on the other, I would not have been able to stand. That random act of kindness and her encouraging words were a great influence.

In 2001, towards the end of my plumbing career, I purchased a fiber optic camera that would enable me to look down sewers and locate septic tanks. It was not widely in use at the time, but I knew that I had to keep pace with technology and always wanted to learn. As a result, I became known as the "sewer proctologist."

5. The Boys

This chapter of my life is dedicated to Robert and John, "the boys." I first met John when I was twelve and he was thirteen. That was when I first came home from Wiltwyck. He was very immature and not very smart. My older sister Kathryn and I attributed his behavior to a head injury caused in a car accident that happened when he was being transported from Wiltwyck to be reunited with our father. The state awarded him $2000 that he would receive at the age of eighteen as compensation.

When he got the money at eighteen, he was infatuated with Trudy Bruce. He spent all two thousand dollars on her. She did not return his affection. He worked in a diner as a short order cook. Even though he functioned at an immature level, he took those orders without missing a beat and always had a big grin on his face.

In 1965, at the age of eighteen, he joined the Army. He completed basic training and was assigned to supply and transportation. He spent one year in Cameron Bay, Viet Nam and received Honorable Discharge on April 29, 1968 after three years of military service.

He was awarded the National Defense Service Medal, the Vietnam Campaign Medal, and the Vietnam Service Medal.

In the summer of 1969, he put on his plastic cowboy boots, a black hat, and his holster holding a cap gun. I asked him where he was going. He replied, "Texas." I thought he would be back by dinner, but he actually went to Texas. Funny, I do not remember anyone asking where he was. Several months later, I got a telephone call from a man named Dick Haney. He told me that John was working on his farm and he was taking care of him. He had been taken advantage of by local hookers who had used his room for their work. John often slept during the day and was up and wondering the streets at night. He did not realize why the women wanted his room. He just thought they needed a room to sleep in. Dick Haney looked after John for seven or eight years. He made sure John was fed and clothed.

The next time I saw John was at my father's funeral in December 1977. This was when I had to become involved in his life. When my father died, I called Dick Haney who gave the news to John. John drove all the way across the country from Texas to New York with no license and no insurance. It was a miracle that he never had an accident or got lost until he got near home. As he got near home, he became confused and drove right through Pine Bush and crashed the car into a grove of trees in Ellenville. He wasn't hurt, but he totaled the car. He was put in jail, and thanks to an understanding sheriff, I was able to get him out in time for the funeral.

After the funeral, I sent him back by bus to Texas. Several years later, in the spring of 1987, I once again got a call from Dick Haney. John had fractured his skull severely in a car accident. He was stumbling and behaving strangely. He seemed to be drunk, but he wasn't. He made wild, erratic movements with his arms and legs. Dick sent him home on a bus, pinning his name and itinerary onto his shirt to be sure he'd make it. We blamed that accident for the irrational behaviors he began to exhibit. It was his second serious head injury. Little did we know it was the beginning of the Huntington's Chorea.

I drove from Albany to meet John at the bus station in Middletown. I managed to get him a small apartment and welfare assistance. Then I didn't see him again until the fall of 1987 when I was contacted by the Orange County Sheriff. John had been picked up for taking food from a grocery store. He was hungry and did not think of it as stealing but only as needing to feed his hunger. There was also a complaint of improper behavior. I was able to secure his release through the judge, but when we returned to his apartment to get his belongings, he ran away. The Middletown police quickly located him and brought him before the same judge who told him that if he did not accompany me to Albany for medical assistance, he would throw the book at him the next time he saw him.

Standing before the judge with John at this time, I was terrified of the responsibility I was taking on. I had no idea what to do next. As John was in the military, I thought if I took him to the Veterans Administration Hospital in Albany that he might receive care there. I was flying by the seat of my pants in handling this matter. On the way to Albany, he tried several times to open the car door because he did not want to go. Because of the impairment of his mind due to Huntington's, it did not register that he might be killed trying to get out of the car. With my cell phone, I called a trooper who was a friend of mine, a sergeant at Exit 23 sub-station, and told him I had my brother with me who was attempting suicide. By using the term "suicide," I felt that we might get immediate care. The trooper met us at the Interchange 23 on the NYS Thruway and suggested that I try the Veteran's Administration. The Veteran's Administration turned John down, as they could not find any injuries related to his military service. Then I took him to the Albany Medical Center Emergency Room. They also turned us away because there were no apparent injuries, and he had no insurance.

It was extremely frustrating trying to handle John and trying to run my plumbing business. One of my customers who worked at a regional mental health facility told me that all I had to do to get him a psychiatric evaluation was to demonstrate that he was a danger to himself or others. Later that week, I chained John to the gate of the governor's mansion in Albany. That got us both arrested. I told the cops that John was threatening to commit suicide. This statement, along with his erratic gait and violent outbursts, got him involuntarily committed to a regional mental health facility. Upon hearing my story, they released me and kept John there from February 15, 1989 until April 6, 1989 for physical and psychological testing. Finally they diagnosed him as having Huntington's chorea. That was the first time I'd ever heard that term. I was totally mystified.

Then there was a screw-up. I found out that John was on a bus headed back to Texas. I called a friend of John's and asked him to put John on a bus back East. He again pinned instructions for John's return and sent him back to New York.

When I investigated why this had happened, I found out that John's psychiatrist was discharged for alleged inappropriate behavior with a client and told to clear all case loads before leaving which resulted in John's early discharge

Outraged, I went to see the administrator. I did not walk, but stormed, into his office. They didn't want to let me in. I told the woman at the desk to call Security; in fact, I told her she'd better call a couple of them. I proceeded to go in. I wasn't "mad," I was totally outraged at what had happened to my brother. I threatened to call the TV stations and air the whole thing about the situation that had been covered up by the administrator unless they would do something immediately for John—such as placing him in an adult care facility. He was returned to the facility on June 16, 1989 for two more months of physical and psychological testing before being transferred on August 18, 1989.

John was placed in the Clermont Adult Care Facility in Tivoli, New York, a residential setting for special needs people. John stayed there for about 18 months.

While John was at the Clermont Home, the residents were taken to Warren Street in Hudson, New York to a facility called the Rip Van Winkle Rehabilitation Center where they were given lunch and went on day trips. One year on my birthday John walked up the street from the Center for Disabilities to a general store and purchased some candles to bring to the birthday party being held for me at the Clermont Home. John did not realize that the candles he had purchased were "joke candles" which automatically re-lit. The home was completely wired with smoke and fire alarm systems which were tied into the local fire department. As the residents gathered around, each with different disabilities, I made my wish and started to blow out the candles. The smoke set off the fire alarms. After gathering up the residents and proceeding outside, we waited for the fire trucks to come. The fire chief, with a good sense of humor, removed each candle one by one from the cake and put them in a bucket of water. The residents enjoyed all the commotion—especially seeing the fire trucks. The firemen stayed and enjoyed some cake. This was one of the last memorable moments before John was permanently placed in a nursing facility.

During 1992, John's body movements became much more erratic. These movements, the wild, erratic, uncontrollable movements of the extremities, were called the "Chorea." The director at the Clermont Home suggested that I move him to a long-term acute care facility. She was concerned about John's going up and down the stairs.

One day, I arrived home around 11:00 pm. My television was on and I heard the words "Huntington's disease." The next day, I called the Channel 6 News Director asking about the previous evening's news clip involving Huntington's disease. From the news director I got the telephone number for the Christian Hill Facility in Lowell, Massachusetts. I called and spoke with Jim Pollard. He suggested that I fly out to Boston and review the facilities and program that he was offering. Christian Hill made the arrangements for a round trip commuter flight from Albany to Boston. I was met by Jim Pollard who introduced me to Paul Ferarra. Together they had created a new Huntington's program.

When I arrived at the facility, I was overwhelmed. In the entrance to the facility there were crystal chandeliers, leather wing back chairs, and fine carpeting. It was beautiful. Jim had to attend a meeting and suggested that I look around and after his meeting we would discuss getting John into the program. I found it to be an immaculately kept facility. I looked in on the physical therapy room and watched as the staff exercised clients. I went through the laundry room and talked with the staff, finding out how long they had been there. Next I made my way to the kitchen and dining room (named the Rose Room) which was very elegant. I checked with all the service departments finding that the staff had been employed for a long time. This told me that the Huntington disease program was being run successfully. The lack of turnover in the staff gave me confidence that it was a well-managed facility. I saw that the staff put their hearts and souls into the care of the patients. I watched the care given as diapers were changed, beds were made, and patients cleaned up for meals. Aides sat with the Huntington's disease patients who were unable to feed themselves. They gently and patiently fed the patients. The curtains, the linens, the leather chairs, and the specialized silverware (constructed so the patient could grip the utensil) were far in excess of what I had expected in a nursing home.

I think in choosing a nursing home, one of the most important things to look at is the staff. If the workers are satisfied and have been on the job for several years, that indicates that the managerial staff is taking care of the employees as well as your family member. I would strongly suggest avoiding a nursing facility (no matter how glamorous it appears), if it has a large turnover of its core people. Don't ever be afraid to express your concerns or fears about how you think your loved one is being cared for. Find a staff that you feel at ease with and with whom you can communicate. You are trusting them with something very valuable—the life of a loved one.

After lunch, we had a meeting in the board room. I indicated that I was more than delighted and hoped that John would be able to transfer to Christian Hill.

I spoke with Jim Pollard about moving John to Christian Hill. Jim called and said that the move was rejected. Columbia County Social Services had approved the transfer, but the State of New York

Department of Health said no. I realized that I would have to light a fire under someone's ass. I knew a plumber who was working in the Capitol building and had access to all the offices. He was able to get me a telephone number that went straight to the Lieutenant Governor's office. I next got the number of a regional supervisor of Health and Human Services in Washington, DC and also the number of the administrator of the regional psychiatric facility in Albany that was treating my brother John Donald Knauer who was suffering from Huntington's disease and was a veteran of the Viet Nam War and deserved better than to die in a gutter. I got them all together on a conference call. I told the person from Washington about New York State's refusal to put John in an out-of-state-facility and that without this care, he would die a premature and hideous death. The administrator from the regional facility confirmed this statement. I told them that if John was not allowed to go to this specialized care, I would sue each person that I was speaking with and their respective agencies. When the gentleman from Washington asked why New York State was not approving John's transfer, they could not give an answer. John needed highly specialized care. New York State did not have a facility with a Huntington's program, and there was an opening at a facility in Lowell, Massachusetts that had a start up program for Huntington's. They agreed to look into the situation and get back to me promptly.

I realized that in order to speak for John, I would have to have Power of Attorney and Power of Physical Care. On July 14, 1992, I got complete legal care of John. I was reluctant to take over John's life and found it emotionally terrifying to take this step. I was able to talk with John, and after going over his options, John was in agreement. I brought my lawyer Carol Stevens over to Clermont.

She had to ask him pertinent questions to determine his mental status. She also had to witness John signing the paper work.

The next thing I knew, I was hearing from Jim Pollard. I will let him tell it in his own words:

> "Years come and go. In fact, many years have come and gone since John came to live at Mediplex of Lowell. As in any other activity, we tend to shape the telling over time. But the way John arrived was so atypical it stands out clearly in my mind.

> People were approved for out-of-state nursing home placement back then by both the State of New York Department of Health and the counterpart health department of the county in which they lived. John's case had won county approval but was denied by the state. It was difficult to determine the criteria that were used by their agents at the time. In retrospect the reason probably was, as ironic as it sounds now, that he was not sick enough! Not yet anyway. At the time he was walking, with very impaired balance, but he was walking. He had difficulty eating but had not choked very often on his food. On and on.

> It was well known to those of us working his case that it was not uncommon to have cases denied placement by the New York Health Department. We were also aware that "all decisions were final." That is, we had never, not once, seen a case that had been denied be

subsequently reconsidered and then approved. We were also aware that it was a paper process and no one had ever received a call from a bureaucrat relevant to any case...ever!

A few days after the denial we had spoken to George about all of the above factors. We had already formed a collaborative bond with George (in retrospect they were the seeds of a lifelong friendship) in our first meeting. He didn't say much at the time beyond a characteristic off-the-cuff "I'll have to put a fire under someone's ass."

A few more days elapse and I get a call from our receptionist who tells me that I have a call from Washington. I ask who it is and she says, "Some government health fellow. He said something about 'Huntington's disease' so I figured it was for you." In the heavily regulated nursing home industry an unexpected call from Washington garners the same reflexive reaction that a flashing blue light in your rear view mirror does on the Northway! I was petrified!

After the gentleman graciously introduced himself with a full set of formal job titles and quick review of how he was responsible for nearly everything related to healthcare in nearly every state east of the Mississippi, I figured I'd better do what I was told. Once I heard the name "John Knauer" I was oriented to why he was calling. It really was a courteous call and he was graciously determined to get John admitted (not just approved) to our facility. I was relieved I hadn't committed a major healthcare violation, excited for John and George and petrified that the wrath of the New York State Health Department would be unleashed on me later.

I explained to him that we would love to have John with us as soon as possible and that we would secure prior approval numbers for billing purposes, arrange an ambulance to take him to us from the Capital District, arrange an attending physician and prepare a room. As it became clear to him that this would take a day or two or three to pull off, as it always did, he asked in that rational but frightening bureaucratic way, "Why can't it happen today?"

I tried to explain that many other people were involved, that there was the matter of distance, required approvals, prior consents and more. He gently insisted that he was in a position to approve every damn thing I could think of and asked me a second time, "So why not later today?"

After about a millisecond of consideration, I said, "Fine, let's do it."

He asked me my name again, how to spell it, my job title and all the relevant details for him to nail down my commitment.

I hung up the phone. There was a flurry of activity. I got a number of so-what-the-fuck-just-happened calls from the corporate office. It put us in a tizzy. I forget if we called George, the Health Department or both right away. I'm sure we did at some point. I also can't remember if John actually arrived later that day. But if he didn't, it was early the next morning. Really, really early.

Epilogue

The sordid details of George's adventure through the bureaucracy were not revealed in detail to me for some time. I asked him to share his story with other families touched by Huntington's disease at a meeting. They never learned a lesson with as much hilarity, but a lesson nonetheless: Love is getting off your ass, fighting city hall, damning the torpedoes and sticking with it.

Me? Hey, what about me? Well, I'm still waiting for the inevitable day the collective wrath of the New York State Health Department is unleashed on me. If it is, they're gonna have to deal with my brother George.

I was stunned when I received Jim's phone call. I had wanted to light a fire, but I didn't expect such blazing immediate action. I did not give the okay to have John moved that day. He needed to say good-bye to all the friends he had made at the Rip Van Winkle Activity Center for mentally and physically handicapped activities.

On Thursday, I brought about one hundred balloons and a cake. We had a party for John's departure.

Friday morning, the day after the party, an ambulette arrived at the Clermont Resident Home at 5:30 a.m. to transport John to Lowell, Massachusetts. Because he did not want to leave, I accompanied the ambulette crew on the three hour ride. The doctor at Clermont suggested that he receive a mild sedative because the health department regulations required that patients being transported must be secured to a gurney. I knew that would be upsetting to him. Most of the time he slept. When he was awake I told him stories of our youth and assured him that he would like where he was going. All the time, I wondered if I was making the right decisions.

When we arrived, I warned the staff not to ask him how he feels. As John was being brought in on a gurney, a nurse made the mistake of asking, "How do you feel?" He proceeded to say, "With my hands," and reached out with both hands to demonstrate. Unfortunately, her breasts got in the way. She then asked, "Where did you come from?" He replied, "From my mother." John was not joking.

John was like a child. I took care of him for over twenty years. He never matured beyond his teens. His economic and personal relationships were far beyond his grasp and comprehension. He was the proverbial "Ever Ready Bunny," smiling and stumbling his way through life as a social outcast.

From 1992 through August 20, 1999, John remained at Mediplex (formerly Christian Hill) in the Huntington's program.

Suzanne Imbriglio, a physical therapist and Director of Rehabilitation at Lowell Health Care Center, Lowell, Massachusetts wrote the following in reference to John. I am including her letter at this point as it illustrates the evolution of treatment for patients with Huntington's disease.

> I first met John in 1992 when he was admitted to the Lowell Health Care Center, then known as Christian Hill. We had begun to treat people with Huntington's disease and we were just learning what strategies would be helpful. There was very little published about the care of people with Huntington's disease. Much of what was in print was psychiatric information which was not very helpful in providing insight into the day to day care of someone with the disease.

> John, like many people with Huntington's disease, was a fighter. He smiled constantly and wanted to "work-out" in the gym. He seemed to not be aware of his many physical limitations. He was determined to keep walking despite frequent falls.

> Physical therapists in those days, rarely worked with people with degenerative disorders. Even cancer patients did not receive Physical Therapy at that time. But I had a lot of experience working with children who had multiple handicaps, mental retardation and even deafness and/or blindness. I knew that the brain could respond and that if the person was motivated, a lot could be done to achieve or maintain function. I approached Huntington's disease in a similar fashion—treating

it like any other chronic illness. While there were no studies to support what I was doing, I began to see some positive results. John, and the other patients like him, began to respond positively to the exercise programs that we initiated. We focused on nutrition as well, and found that improving a person's weight, improved their overall physical functioning as well as their mood. We instituted high calorie snacks as part of the daily routine and watched as our patients actually improved.

Gym became part of the daily routine as well, and many of the patients maintained their ability to walk for much longer than those patients who did not participate in such activities.

Today, while there are still no clinical studies to support these ideas, a study done on mice that received enhanced nutrition and exercise outlived other mice with Huntington's disease that did not received the enriched environment. We now know that keeping a person's weight 5-10% above ideal body weight helps to reduce chorea and enhances functional performance. Keeping a person active both mentally and physically also serves to slow the progression of the disease and allows the person to better adjust to the changes that occur with the disease process. We are also doing a better job of identifying depression and aggressively treating it so that people suffer much less from the emotional component of the disease.

John was so helpful in our learning process of Huntington's disease. He was usually agreeable to trying new equipment such as walkers or helmets and different beds to promote safety. Without people like John, we would have never achieved the skills that we have today.

I went there twice a week for about six to eight months, leaving at 3:00 p.m. for the three hour ride to Lowell Massachusetts and getting home about 3:00 a.m. John was still in the habit of sleeping during the day and wandering the halls at night. I wanted to help John change his sleeping pattern and participate in daytime programs. I used mostly bribes to manipulate him. To keep him awake during the day, we went to Dunkin' Donuts in downtown Lowell and got several chocolate donuts. He loved everything and anything that was chocolate. To see him smile with a mouth full of chocolate donut made everything that I did worthwhile.

My truck had a cell phone mounted on the floor. Once in awhile, we would call our sister Rosemary. On her birthday, we would sing "Happy Birthday" to her. We would also go to a Mall where we walked around seeing the different shops. The main reasons for doing this were to keep him active, to maintain the muscles in his legs, and to keep his mind active. He enjoyed toy and pet shops. One day we went to Sears to purchase bar bells and weights to be used at his facility. John enjoyed participating in facility activities, and when something was needed, I would take him to the store and let him pick things out. I wanted him to be a part of his own welfare. Many times, people would stand back as we walked. John's erratic movements had people thinking that he might be drunk or on drugs. By my seeing him so often, he was able to adjust to the new facility.

During the summer months, while John was still able to walk, he attended a special summer camp for a week. The times spent at summer camp were the last thing that he was able to do on his own before needing the assistance of a walker. My sister Rosemary and I set up his walker with a bicycle basket and a horn. In the six months that he used the walker, he drove the staff crazy beeping his little horn.

As his health declined, he went from being ambulatory, to using a walker, to being in an ordinary wheel chair, and finally to being in a Broda chair. The Broda is a specially constructed wheel chair which supported his body but limited his movements. Every stage of John's deterioration was difficult because John did not understand that his physical body could not do what it had always done. His mind never caught up with his illness. I was there for each one of these steps to reassure him. He never understood that he was dying. He would always say, "My equilibrium is off."

During the seven years that John was at Mediplex, I attended seminars on Huntington's. Health care professionals, family members, and lawyers gathered for the workshops. In the evenings, there was a banquet where department heads, dieticians, physical therapists, and family could interact with each other informally. I learned that Huntington's was the first genetic marker discovered in 1992 which allowed direct blood testing to find out if a person carried the gene and would develop Huntington's. I learned about the legal ramifications and how to advocate on the behalf of the patient. Everything I learned in the process of caring for John helped me to take care of Robert when he developed the disease. I never dreamed that the things I was learning would be needed later.

After John settled in, I was able to cut back my visits to several times a month. Each time I went to visit him, I would bring extra treats so that John could share with others. Many patients had no visitors. Over the years, I "pseudo-adopted" several of these patients.

Every Tuesday for eighteen years, no matter which facility he was in, I arranged for the staff to have John telephone me at 8:00 p.m. There were times that John could mumble something that I could understand but most times he was not articulate. Having him make these phone calls made him feel special. Over time, a ritual developed. I would say key phrases such as "Mama Mia" to which he would respond "Spicy meat ball," or I would ask if he had been a good boy. He would answer, "Bad Boy. Have more fun." These phrases let me know where John was mentally and gave me a gauge of his decline. Sometimes, I would ask questions to keep his mind focused, such as the names of his siblings, or what we did as kids. Other times when I asked him how old he was, he would say he was anything from a hundred to a million years old. At times when he would get upset, he would holler at the nurse to call his "ugly brother." Thus another name I had for John was "Handsome." These were signals that his connection to reality was slipping. Huntington's ravishes the mind long before it deteriorates the body.

When John was confined to a wheel chair, I would often take him out for walks. His wheel chair became his "Golden Chariot."

During the years, John was moved many times. First he was at the Clermont Facility until he could no longer manage the stairs. He was then transferred to Lowell, Massachusetts. The ownership at Lowell changed hands several times and the quality of care deteriorated. Jim Pollard left to establish a facility at Laurel Lake in Lee, Massachusetts with a dedicated section for Huntington's patients. John was moved to Laurel Lake on August 20, 1999. I moved John myself for the last time. I felt that he would have a better time if he went in my truck. I picked up some donuts, lined the truck's front seat with bed pads, and off we went.

In November 2000, the Guthrie Center hosted a luncheon at the famous "Alice's Restaurant." Arlo Guthrie's mother died in 1967 from the effects of Huntington's disease. Arlo Guthrie brought together patients from the Laurel Lake Center and many scientists who were researching the disease. Jim Pollard asked me to bring John to the Thanksgiving luncheon while others were brought by the facility's van. John was the only patient who had family at the luncheon. John beamed as he rode in my truck and again when he was interviewed by Channel 13 and *Albany Times Union* newspaper. I did most of the talking as John's speech was garbled, but he enjoyed the attention. I had never shared information about my family with my community. When the newspaper article and television segment came out, many community members commented on the interviews and told me what a great thing it was that I was caring for John. I had never thought of what I was doing as "a great thing." I had a good life, a home, a business, a Harley, and I was healthy. John was the hero. He was bravely facing the ravishes of Huntington's and slowly dying.

In the summer of 2001, the program director at Laurel Lake called and asked me to help bring John and five other Huntington's patients to Yankee Stadium. They had a nurse and an aide available but needed another person to assist. I went, taking care of John and one other patient. I was able to do the heavy lifting, carrying the coolers and loading and unloading the wheel chairs. We divided the care and feeding of the patients. Yankee Stadium has a special section dedicated for handicapped people. We were in the far out-field. The stadium's personnel were exceptional getting us to our seats. There were three marvelous moments at the stadium. First, a sign welcoming the people from Laurel Lake appeared on the electronic billboard. Next, during one of the innings, Derek Jeeter, who was playing the outfield, came to our area and tossed his cap up to us. The third moment was when the organ played "Take me out to the ball game." The patients, who were not really aware of their surroundings, came alive and began trying to sing along and waving their arms.

The following year, when we went to Yankee Stadium, we were allowed to take the patients onto the field to the memorial wall where former Yankee greats are honored. While we were there, Derek Jeeter came over and shook hands with each one of the patients.

Up to this point, I was only taking care of John, and then Robert needed my care. In 1961 when I came home from Wiltwyck, Robert was about eight years old. I found no structure to live by. There was utter chaos and living conditions were deplorable. My father would come home after work and go into the living room with a full bottle of Schaeffer beer to relax for the evening. After he fell asleep, Robert would polish off what was left in the bottle and often became drunk. I knew that something was terribly wrong with my family.

This is when I first started to assume responsibilities for situations that were not of my making. I hitchhiked twenty-five miles to Goshen, the county seat, to get help. I really did not know what I was going to do when I got there, but I knew that was where social services were located. After knocking on many doors, I found a woman who was in charge of Family Services. I tried to explain to her what was happening and asked her to look into it. I then headed back home. By the time I got home, someone had contacted my father. Needless to say, I got a beating. At that age, I knew that I could fight back, but out of respect I stood there and took what my father handed out. I was very conflicted about having gone to Social Services. I was not sure that I had done the right thing. After all this, there was no follow through by Social Services other than the call to my father to let him know that I had registered my concerns.

I do not know much about Robert's youth because I spent most of my childhood living at Wiltwyck School for Boys and later living with my friend Charlie's family. Most of what I learned came from my Aunt Tootsie. Robert grew up without much supervision and seemed to make his own rules. Alcohol and assorted narcotics took over his life.

One day when Robert was about eighteen years old, he "borrowed" our older brother Arthur's shot gun and shells. Robert got drunk, went home, and began to blast out windows and doors. Ken Henry, the police officer called to Robert to put the shot gun down. As Ken Henry looked inside to see where Robert was located, Robert pointed the shot gun at Ken Henry's ear and pulled the trigger. Luckily, there were no more shells in the chamber of the gun. Why Ken Henry did not fire his pistol at Robert is something that only he and God know. The reason Robert gave for blasting holes in the apartment was that it was too hot in the house. This was only one example of his spiraling out of control.

He spent about seven years in the county jail at periodic six to nine month stretches for being drunk and disorderly, barroom brawls, and acquiring cars to ride in that were not his. He had frequent disagreements with the county welfare system which also led to short periods of incarceration for fraud. Several times he "borrowed" the local school buses for a joy ride. As these episodes progressed, he transformed from an innocent child to a man who could be meaner than a junk yard dog. He was just a six-foot tall mean son of a bitch.

One of the last times Robert was in jail was in Ulster County. A deputy sheriff had caught him driving a car that he took from a bar. When he was caught, he said, "I was just borrowing it." I do not think he ever got a legal license. I went down to the jail in Kingston, New York. He swore that he had not done it. I swore that I would never be back as long as he was going to die. But yet again, I did go back to help. I couldn't find it in my heart to blame him for his drinking and drug abuse. He was a product of his environment.

Robert lived with May Lynn Enderly, his common-law wife, in Pine Bush, New York and their son, Robert Michael Knauer, Jr. The house that they lived in was absolutely filthy. Robert never worked for a living. He was on welfare and May worked on a horse farm. Symptoms of Huntington's disease had started already.

After May died of a heart attack, her mother raised Robert Jr. and cared for Robert Sr. When she died in the same year of pneumonia, Robert called me. After getting off the phone with Robert, I knew I had to do something. I immediately called the State Police to do a "health and welfare" check on Robert and his son. When they arrived at the house, on November 21, 1998, one officer "lost his lunch" due to the stench. Robert Michael Jr. was taken into protective custody. Robert Sr. was arrested under mental health law and put in lockdown at Arden Hill Hospital's mental health ward. Later Robert Michael Jr. was placed with an uncle where he remained until his eighteenth birthday.

At Arden Hill, in Goshen, New York, Robert got physiological and psychological screenings. He was discharged on December 10, 1998 and transferred to Heritage House, an adult acute-care living facility in Middletown, New York. Robert was placed there so that he was approximately five miles away from his son. Unfortunately, visits never materialized.

On March 24, 2002, while eating a hot dog, Robert coughed. He swallowed his lower denture which lodged in his throat. I got an emergency page at 9:00 p.m. from Horton Hospital, in Middletown, New York. They needed my permission to do the surgery as I had his Health Care Proxy. It was about ten minutes before I could get to a landline. By the time I got to the phone, they had already performed the emergency surgery as the situation was a matter of life or death. I knew that I had to get there as soon as possible as Robert would not be cooperative. When I reached his bedside, he was awakening from the anesthesia. He was not happy and was violent both verbally and physically. He had a nurse in each hand and had ripped out his IV out. There was blood all over the place. Luckily, I was able to calm him down by bellowing some expletives in a voice that could be heard throughout the hospital.

I telephoned Jim Pollard the next day to fill him in on what was happening. Jim was holding the last opening for the placement of Robert so that he could be with John in the same facility. Jim needed to get county and New York State approval for funding before the transfer could be made.

On March 30, 2002, Jim Pollard came to see Robert at Horton Hospital. He was able to re-enforce my opinion from a professional stand point that Robert needed specialized care.

This is how Jim described the encounter with Robert:

I recall meeting Robert for the first time. I had heard about him from George and his stay at an adult home. George, contrasting Robert's personality to John's, had described him as "meaner than a junk yard dog." He had hunkered down in his room at the home and only ventured out to get junk food and other essentials. As time went by, George preferred to have him in a safer setting with John at Laurel Lake nursing home. Inevitably the call came one day from a community hospital in the Middletown area. Robert had swallowed his dentures and they had lodged in his esophagus or windpipe requiring surgical removal. On arrival at the hospital, I had no idea what type of personality that I would find. The image of someone "meaner than a junkyard dog," the discomfort that I presumed came with swallowing a denture, and the typically short temper that comes with Huntington's prepared me to meet a very angry fellow.

When I walked into the room I was struck by how thin he was lying in his hospital bed. Having seen old photos of Robert, he had been a big guy, bigger than both George and John in the pictures. He smiled and was very gentle when I greeted him. His handshake was weak and his personality was accommodating. He recounted accurately his dental misfortune and, other than being sore from the procedure to remove it, was in good spirits. Evidently, Huntington's disease had tempered his personality a great deal. He was eating small bites of a sandwich and sipped flattened hospital ginger ale through a straw. He certainly wasn't excited about coming to, as he called it, "a nursing home." On some level, though, he appeared to have resigned himself to not returning to the adult home. When I asked him where he was going after his hospital stay, he said "back to my room" in the adult home. He never objected to suggestions that it would be unsafe there and that it was not a realistic option.

As I was leaving I suspected that he was overly gracious with me and that he would be more resistant to placement at Laurel Lake as time went on. But I do not recall the intransigence about staying in Middletown that I had suspected.

The reason Jim does not recall his "intransigence" was that before contacting Jim I had a rather forceful discussion with Robert.

When Robert was discharged on March 28, 2002, he was no longer appropriate for Heritage House and needed more specialized care. I consulted with the attending physician and let him know that I had planned to place Robert at Laurel Lake and required the discharge paper work to be written up in such a manner that New York State would see the necessity of having him transferred to a dedicated facility for Huntington's. The doctor wrote the order so that he was placed temporarily in Middletown Park Manor, a full service nursing home.

Before I could place Robert at Laurel Lake, I was struck, on

April 14, 2002, by a sudden, almost fatal illness that took my sight but spared my life. I was still in charge of Robert's care and was the only one who knew where he was and had the legal authority to move him.

On April 25, after I came out of my coma, I called Jim Pollard to update him about what had happened. Jim then made the arrangements for transferring him to Laurel Lake. On May 1, 2002, he was taken by ambulette and admitted to Laurel Lake in Lee, Massachusetts where he remained until his death.

With John and Robert now both at Laurel Lake facility, one hour away from Coxsackie, I knew they were getting the proper care. They were under the supervision of Jim Pollard, and that was a great comfort to me.

Both John and Robert were very heavy smokers and could not be persuaded to stop. I tried bribing them with treats. When that did not work, I promised them that if instead of their usual eight cigarettes a day, they would cut down to four cigarettes, I would give them a color TV with a built-in VCR for cartoons and I would pay their cable bill. I'll be dammed if they didn't both stop smoking entirely. They got their promised rewards.

Again, I will use an excerpt from Jim's letter:

> Healthcare staff tends to presume that brothers share a lifetime of fraternal goodwill and a profound friendship when they come into residential settings. This is commonly not the case, and John and Robert were no exception. They never had issues at the nursing home. But it appeared that their lives with each other in the nursing home had more significance to George

and the staff than it did to John and Robert. For the first few weeks after Robert's admission, John visited his room daily sitting in his wheelchair next to his brother's bed. The advanced cognitive features of Huntington's disease render it virtually impossible to have a true conversation, one with back and forth comments and questions. There was no conversing beyond occasional comments. But John gave it a good effort. Robert, being more socially passive at this time, appeared to welcome his moments with John but would never initiate them. Given their natures, it's no surprise that John was more active at trying to connect with him.

As time went on, the staff and I saw that Robert really was not going to be an active participant in any of the activities that went on daily. Where John would only miss a session if he was too sick to attend, Robert would have no part of them. He reluctantly agreed a few times to check them out. This only served to confirm for him that he did, in fact, want no part of the activities. He commented that he didn't want to "go to school again" and it was "baby stuff." In fact, the activities were very age-appropriate and fun for those who came as they reviewed winning Lotto numbers, baseball scores, NASCAR results, soap opera story lines and other events of the day. Just as he had at the adult home, it was clear that Robert would hunker down in his room and only leave when he wanted something. Again, unlike John, who would only be found in his room sleeping or intently watching a specific TV show or cartoon video.

The staff never gave up trying to involve Robert in the activity of the nursing home. But we failed. You couldn't finish an invitation to anything that was going on before he'd gently say "no." It was frustrating when he'd smile as he said it. We'd often go into his room intent on just getting him up out of bed to walk around the building. We thought that he might be more amenable to participating if he just saw what was going on. Despite the effort and good intention, Robert graciously rejected nearly every offer, intent on spending his days in his room.

In retrospect, his first few weeks set the stage for the rest of his life, preferring to spend his time primarily in his room, opting out of participation in the day-to-day life of the home and forgoing relationships with fellow residents and staff. Huntington's disease had transformed his meanness into apathy. As time would show, Robert was gently passive in the face of his progressive loss and disability. John was ever the "damn the torpedoes" warrior. Different as their approaches were, both shared a grace and ease as their course of HD unfolded.

As the months went by, Robert ate less and less and the pounds melted off his already thin frame. He neither refused the delivery of a meal nor showed impatience with those trying to convince him to eat at least a portion of his meal. Dietary supplements, in the form of high calorie milk shakes, were added to his diet. At the end of a day, despite his constant reassurances that he would drink them, three or four were left untouched on his bedside table. He'd tell staff that he preferred them at room temperature and that he'd drink them when they warmed up. An efficient way to escape the ongoing nagging to eat what the staff delivered.

He continued to lose weight and he took on a "skin and bones" appearance with the frailty that came with it. His rib cage protruded from his trunk in very vivid contrast to the photo of him, stocky and muscular, that John had in his room. An unfamiliar person would never be convinced that they were the same person.

It is essential that Huntington's patients be put on diet high in fats and carbohydrates. Their metabolism, even while they are asleep, is burning calories at three times the normal rate. Over time, because of their decreasing ability to swallow, their diet goes from solids to pureed food. When I went to visit and found out that they were not eating enough, I would sit down by their sides, sometimes gently coaxing them and other times threatening them with my cane. Even though I was blind, somehow I was able to bring my cane up near their faces without touching them. They never realized that I was blind.

In May 2004, Robert had all his remaining teeth extracted. With the bribery of Reese's Peanut Butter Cups, he was encouraged to eat. Robert had deteriorated much more rapidly, physically and mentally, than John. His weight loss was extreme and his speech had become unintelligible.

On June 28, 2004, I got a call from the nursing home. Both boys were at a dangerous point from which they would never recover. Death was creeping closer and closer. Both had lost a lot of weight and were having a very hard time eating. That evening, John had to be put on oxygen.

I insisted, with great trepidation, that there would be no feeding tube for either of the boys. A feeding tube would have extended their physical existence, but there would be no quality of life for them. They would not be able to enjoy that life. There would be just the shell of a body being fed and diapered. The weight of the decisions I had to make was sometimes crushing. At times I wished I could pass it on to others or walk away from it, but I couldn't. My siblings were unable and unwilling to share the burden. I prayed that I was making the right choices for the boys.

During the night of June 29, 2004, I got a call from the nursing home. Robert had gone to the nursing station and indicated that he wanted to call me. Jim Pollard thought that if he were moved from the Huntington's ward to another part of the nursing home where people were more active, he might eat better. Even though Robert couldn't articulate, he muttered into the phone, "eating, eating," and I knew what he wanted was not to be moved. I called the nursing home on June 30, 2004 and told them he was not to be moved and if he died as a result, so be it. I prayed, "God help me if I am wrong."

During the next couple of months, I went out to visit both John and Robert and could see their decline. I realized that Robert was near death; his stomach was sucked in almost to his back bone. He was eating very little and existed on the Ensures they got him to drink.

One might think that because I am blind, I would not be able to see how skeletal Robert had become. I could see more poignant changes unsighted then many sighted people could. I held Robert's back and stomach between my thumb and pinkie. He was so close to death that it seemed like he was awaiting it with open arms. I prayed that God would take him in his sleep.

I hear politicians talk about the morality of stem cell research. They are not the ones witnessing family members living with such things as Huntington's, Parkinson's disease, spinal injuries, blindness, and many other afflictions. I do not see the President, Vice President, Governor, or any political leaders visiting a nursing facility. Yet they feel moral indignation and slow the progress of science.

At the end of August, I made the decision that I wanted all medications stopped for Robert. His attending physician agreed to wean him off his medications and just give him comfort care.

On September 10, I met with the nursing supervisor, director of Laurel Lake, the attending physician, and Jim Pollard. They wanted to put Robert on a feeding tube. I finally lost my temper. I had anguished over these decisions about Robert and John. I did not want their suffering to be prolonged. Robert and John were to be made comfortable without feeding tubes or by other artificial means. I felt that I had to fight on behalf of my brothers. At the end of the meeting, I knew that they were not on the same page with me. The first thing I did when I got home was to telephone the owner of Laurel Lake, Craig Blessing. Craig's father was also a Huntington's patient and he understood where I was coming from. He said, "I will take care of it." That was the last of any interference.

I noticed on that same visit that John was slumping in his wheel chair. His upper torso was leaning to the right, cutting off his breathing. He was choking on his own saliva because he could no longer keep his chin off of his chest. He had fallen out of his wheel chair several times and had to be taken to Berkshire Medical for stitches. I believed that John needed to be taken out of the wheel chair immediately and placed in a Broda chair. A Broda chair is a reclining wheel chair. The patient's body and head can be centered with support from pillow pads on either side of the chair. The staff did not want to make the change. I was so irate that my blood pressure shot through the roof. I angrily and unapologetically demanded that my decisions were not be challenged and to be implemented immediately. When I left the building, I was so frustrated and angry I cried all the way home.

After John was put in the Broda chair, they realized that I was right. Sometimes, the patient's advocate must stand behind what he feels or senses. I was certain that I needed to intercede on Robert and John's behalf and insisted that my decisions be implemented. After we switched John from a conventional wheel chair to a Broda chair, he could no longer use his feet or hands to push or guide himself along. He had to be pushed along by someone to get to every event. Safety cushions were placed to keep his body centered and from slipping out of the chair.

I had demanded that John be routinely removed from his chair shortly after lunch and put down for a nap. Initially, he was upset because it broke his routine. In the afternoons when he was put back in his chair, he became much more compliant with his medications and his evening feeding. On January 20, 2006, about a year after their deaths, I heard from Sarah Miller of Laurel Lake. The nursing home has instituted a policy of putting other Huntington's patients down for a nap, relieving them of the long arduous day of being wheelchair-bound. This procedure has shown a marked improvement in disposition and decreased mood swings of the patients.

I noticed that as the Huntington's progressed, the boys who once spoke with clear, strong voices now spoke imperceptibly in utter mutter. It was as frustrating for me to understand as it was for them in communicating. Their inability to communicate increased their frustration and anger. I found if I pretended to understand what they were saying, it eased their burden. Their communications were often only a wiggle, a giggle, a grunt, or a moan, but they knew I was there, and it made them smile.

On Sunday, September 12, 2004, the day before John was put in the Broda chair, my friend Anne and I went to see the boys at Laurel Lake. It was a beautiful, sunny autumn day. We decided to take both John and Robert for a ride in their wheel chairs around the outside of the facility. Anne led the way pushing Robert, and I brought up the rear pushing John. We must have looked like a train in motion. I was able to follow her voice and slight guidance of "right," "left," or "straight." The boys had on their special blue jackets that I had had made up for them. John's had the name of "Bad Boy" sewn on it (because "Bad boys have more fun") and Robert's jacket said "Tough Guy" (because he was "meaner than a junk yard dog.") My jacket simply read "George." As we pushed

John and Robert around the building facility, the two gladiators sat proudly in their chariots as they were whisked around on their final journey together.

After making the round of the facility, we rested outside of the front entrance to soak up the sun's warm rays. This was the final time that the three of us were together as brothers. It was a defining moment. I knew that all of the decisions I had made were for the best. My soul was comforted. We were all at peace with the knowledge that these were their final days. It was to be only five weeks later that death gently retrieved Robert from his earthly commitments.

It was fortunate that I had previously cultivated a personal relationship with Jim Pollard and Sarah Miller. After my sudden illness and blindness, I was unable to go to the facility for about ten months. During this time I was undergoing intensive physical and mental rehabilitation. I could rely on their commitment and care for Robert and John. They were my eyes and ears at the nursing home, and I made decisions based on what they reported to me daily.

On the fourteenth of October, I received a shocking call from the nursing home. I had asked them to do weekly weights. For the past two and a half months, Robert had been around one hundred and twenty pounds. His weight was now one hundred and seven. I prayed that God would take him fast. It ripped my heart hearing his weight. Robert had not gotten up in two days. I met with Jim Pollard, Sarah, and Dr. Kaplan and they felt that Robert would live for several weeks. Jim was surprised that he was still there.

While writing about this part of my brothers' stories, I asked Jim Pollard for some help in telling about Robert's last days. Jim wrote:

George ramped up his constant monitoring to vigilance. Thinking that I had a bit of influence with Robert, I tried personally to convince him to eat. One of my approaches was to ask him, "If you could have anything to eat, what would it be?" He replied, "A hamburger." I asked him how he wanted it cooked. I got up to go to the kitchen where the chef would cook him, literally, whatever he wanted. I wasn't out the door of his room when he said, "Tomorrow." I thought I had gotten somewhere and screamed silently to myself.

I went to the kitchen anyway, and the chef cooked me a hamburger. Since he knew Robert's story, he molded a huge hamburger out of ground beef instead of a frozen hamburger patty. It looked great. He even took an electric knife and sliced the edges so it would still look appetizing but would be easier to bite. He plated it with pickles, lettuce, tomatoes, and cole slaw. It looked the "Hamburger Deluxe" in a New York style diner! The chef agreed to give me five minutes with him before he would come to Robert's room, in chef's hat and white coat, to ask him if it was okay.

Five minutes later, the chef arrived to find me talking about hamburgers with Robert and the plate untouched on his bedside table. A chef from the Ritz-Carlton couldn't have done a better job at kissing his butt to see if there was any conceivable thing he could do to that hamburger to get him to eat it. "No. No. No.

No." To every question he'd answer "No." Of course, he smiled appreciatively when he rejected every question or suggestion. This was the first of several tries, every one of them unsuccessful.

A few days later, it was a McDonald's cheeseburger. I sat with him, broke it into small pieces at his request, and he ate about half of it. The next day I did the same thing. I left him alone and watched him discreetly from the hallway as he ate about three bites of it. Back in the room, I convinced him to try a few more. He did, but it still wasn't finished. Now, I know that those last few bites exhausted any influence I had with him.

He was so frail it looked like a common hug would collapse his rib cage. He could walk, but it was too risky lest he fall. He would dress less often, content to spend his days in a Johnny {diaper} and sweat pants with an elastic waist band. George had several "intense discussions" with him about eating. Over time, they subtly changed from exhortations to eat and reasons to keep fighting into compassionate preparations for the end of his life. George talked to him about his son in Florida and life in general. It's hard to tell what Robert understood. On some level, though, I bet he did.

Guiding Robert through the last few months of his life was draining for George. But Robert never said "No" to George's involvement and stewardship. He may never have said "Yes" either. But given the cognitive ravages of Huntington's disease, his simple acquies- cence to all that George did was as loud a "Yes" as one could reasonably expect and as articulate an expression of gratitude as he could muster.

October 21, 2004, Anne and I went over to the nursing home to see Robert for the last time and stayed for about one hour. Robert had had nothing to eat or drink for forty-eight hours. I found that he had lost another fifteen pounds and weighed about eighty-five to ninety pounds. His bones and ribs were protruding; he could barely breathe and could only whimper. As I sat there at his bedside and prayed for him, I was afraid to touch him or try to move him. Anne, who was standing in the doorway, noticed that Robert had moved his left arm and placed it across his body so that I could hold his hand. She told me what had happened and I took Robert's hand. I told him that his son, Robert Michael Knauer, Jr., had graduated high school and that I would be notify him of his passing. I stroked his fingers and told him gently that it was time to let go. There was a change in Robert's breathing—it became quieter. He was slowly slipping into his chair at God's table.

As we were leaving Laurel Lake, one of the nurses said to Anne that it was so nice that I could be there with my brother—many patients die alone. Shortly after I arrived home, Laurel Lake tele- phoned me that Robert had passed on. Although it was very hard for me, I was at peace that I had been with him in his last moments.

Before I went blind, I thought that I had seen all the ugliness that life can give. You would think that, now, living in total black- ness, I would be immune from life's ugliness, but that is not the case. My father had been killed in a factory fire along with his faithful dog. When I took the charred remains of his dog to be buried, I removed the body from the canvas it had been wrapped in. The sight horrified me. I imagined what my father's body must have looked like. That image has haunted me. Now, being blind, as I used my fingers, the lenses to my mind, to tactile Robert's skeletal frame, I was as horrified as I was then. Robert had been a six foot, 300 pound man only six years to the day earlier, and on the day of his death he weighed 85 pounds.

On October 22, 2004, I contacted my remaining siblings, Rosemary, Kathleen, and Arthur, notifying them of Robert's passing. Months later I was able to locate Robert Jr. and notified him of his father's death.

Michael Lobb of Brady's Funeral Home made all the necessary arrangements to have Robert cremated and interred at the Prospect Cemetery in Pine Bush, New York. On November 10, 2004, we placed him in the plot where our father was buried. It was almost six years to the day that I had begun the journey with him. Now he rests, less than a mile from his home. Finally he is at peace.

I had to borrow money to bury him. I had no assistance from any of my siblings in making arrangements. It saddened me that even at his death they remained indifferent and unconcerned. Joe Ann, a good friend of mine, flew up from Delaware to attend the funeral, but some of my own siblings didn't come. Joe Ann honored my brothers by providing their bronze grave markers. It was a very cold and gray morning when we buried Robert. Only my sister Rosemary, her husband Guy, my brother Arthur with his children, Art and Christina, and my extended family, the Hancock's were at the grave side. The Pastor's eulogy was so eloquent that my anger faded from me. The sun came out from under the clouds as the preacher began to speak and as I felt the sun at the back of my neck, I was at peace.

John remained at Laurel Lake, but Huntington's disease was taking its toll on him. June 21, 2005, Arthur and I went over to see him and found his health declining.

On June 23, 2005, I talked to Dr. Falstein and Jim Pollard, requesting that all medications be stopped except ones that would provide comfort care. They concurred with my decision.

I was able to visit John every other week and found that he was the proverbial "Every Ready Bunny" with ups and downs. He loved to please the nurses and me.

When I began to write this book, I asked Jim Pollard and Sarah Miller to write about their memories of John and Robert. On October 24, 2005, I received an e-mail from Sarah Miller who took care of John and is now Program Manager for the Huntington's program at Laurel Lake. Sarah was wonderful with both of my brothers and I completely trusted and relied on her. The following shows the wonderful care John received and also how difficult that care giving was. This is what she wrote:

> "I fed John this morning in one of our classes. He did well; his swallowing was stable and he did not lose much food. He also ate all of his lunch and was asking for more. I went to the kitchen and got him more. He gets double portions of food with all meals. He was hungry today. He still had some drainage but not as bad as before. His nose had to be wiped one or two times during lunch but not at all in our morning classes. It has

been a great pleasure for me to work with both John and Robert. I miss Robert and wish I was able to know him longer. It has been five years with John and counting. I am thankful for the opportunity. I am also thankful for you too, George. Family members that take care of their loved ones truly are the experts. I have really learned a lot from you. You are extremely dedicated, loyal and strong. I will talk to you soon.

Thank You
Sarah

By September, 2005, Julius Caesar could no longer ride his chariot on a warm summer day around the outside of the nursing home. The ride that he and I had taken countless times came to an end, for the fiendish dragon of death was slowly, painfully, and torturously bringing John's life to an end. As John's death grew close, I would awaken during the night in a terrible fright and call the nursing home only to be reassured that John was resting comfortably.

About the beginning of February 2006, Anne and I drove over to see John. During our visit, John was pointing with his left hand toward his abdomen. This was strange for John to do, so Anne picked up his shirt to see if there was a rash or anything else that might be bothering him. She saw nothing. It was not until I ran my fingers across his stomach that I realized his stomach was hard and extended. I started to question John. John could communicate, but you had to listen to his sounds and interpret them. We came to the conclusion that John may have been constipated. I had set up a system years ago that anytime John went to the bathroom, his bowel movements would be recorded. The record sheet showed that he had had two moderate movements in the past two days. This indicated that his body was functioning, but yet something was wrong. I told Debbie Richardson, Laurel Lake Administrator, and Sarah Miller, about his hard, extended stomach and complaints of pain. Even with my insistence, it took them two days to take John to the Berkshire Hospital. X-rays showed that his system was completely impacted. For some unknown reason, instead of cleaning him out while at the hospital, they sent John back to Laurel Lake where the personnel were not prepared to use the procedures recommended by the hospital as they did not have the supplies. With soap enemas and suppositories a little was cleaned out, but he was still impacted. They used a KUB (ultrasound) several times but only saw minimal results.

Even with the knowledge that John was completely impacted, the aids feeding John commented that he was not eating very much. They failed to figure out that it is hard to put anything into a full container. It is important that people with Huntington's disease eat to maintain a healthy body, as the disease uses up excessive energy. John's weight had dropped and I feared that his body was starting to shut down.

Again, I insisted that a surgical consult be arranged with a doctor and the best that they could do was four days later. I had kept telephone numbers of people in charge of the New York and Massachusetts health care systems, and I used them. Making these calls was the only way to get a doctor in to see John. The first doctor came for about fifteen minutes and said that he was impacted and that there was really not too much to be done except to continue with enemas and suppositories as this was going to continue to happen again.

Upon speaking with the doctor and hearing his attitude, I insisted that John's doctor be changed. Dr. Wespiser was brought in on a Friday evening. He was gentle with John and was able to remove excrement that he said amounted to the size of three grapefruits. He realized that John's body was shutting down and his system required immediate assistance in order for John to maintain a level of comfort.

Two days prior to John's passing, I went over to see him with my friends, Charlie and Patti Hancock. John seemed very quiet. The next day, Rosemary, Arthur, Guy and my friend Gina went to visit. John was in great spirits, smiling and enjoying their company.

John slipped from man's world into God's world on Sunday, March 26, 2006 at 10:00 p.m. After John's death, his ashes were in my home. While I mourned and began his chapter in this book, I asked Jim to write about his memories of John.

"Remembering John"

In the last three years of his life John lost his ability to walk by himself. This was due to impaired balance and the tightness in his legs brought on by Huntington's disease which caused changes in his muscle tone. He used his wheelchair to get around the building. It slowed him down a bit in the beginning and a lot as the years went by. When he first used his wheelchair, he propelled it by gripping and pushing the wheels. Then, as that became more difficult and less efficient, he would propel it backwards with his feet and legs. It may have been more or less a zigzag down a long corridor bumping into a wall now and then, but it worked well enough for him to do it without asking or waiting for help. He always, until the very end, knew where he wanted to be and somehow he got there on his own.

I point this out because John always did whatever he could do for himself. As physically impaired as he may have been at any time, he never lost his single-minded determination to focus on where he wanted to go and to get there using whatever skill he had left to do it. Professionals talk about assisting disabled people to maintain their independence; sometimes it serves only as a well-intentioned lofty goal. Never in John's case, though. He struggled push by push, turn by turn, and moment to moment to do whatever he had set his mind on. He might have needed to be reminded that something was happening somewhere and pointed along his way, but he would rather push himself there than get a lift from the staff. Sometimes we'd feel guilty because we could easily save him great effort and get him there on time. But, he'd make it clear with a simple "No!" or an expression that was half smile and half scowl that said, "I'll do it myself." I always admired this.

In his last few years, his legs were stiffer and more rigid. When he stood up, his two legs would go straight and it would take some time and relaxation to get them to bend at his knees. This made it easier for us to help him out of his chair and onto the toilet or into bed because his straight legs made it easy for him to pivot around as we grabbed him in a bear hug.

When he wanted to go to the bathroom, he'd look up from underneath his padded helmet and use an open palm to motion to his crotch. He'd use the expression left in his face to let his helpers know whether or not he simply had to use the bathroom or if we had to rush to the bathroom. The rush to "pee" was frantic at times, but he loved the fun of being whisked away full tilt to the bathroom. This didn't help him hold his bladder, but he'd laugh like hell.

It was always a pleasure to help him in the bathroom because he knew what he could do and what he couldn't do any more for himself. Once his wheelchair was in the bathroom with the door now closed, you'd simply ask him, "What do you want me to do?" If he wanted help with his pants, he'd signal pushing them down by looking at his crotch and trying to tug at them with an open rigid palm. Other times, he'd want you to help him stand and pivot onto the toilet and would signal that by stretching both arms up to you. Other times, he'd reach to the wall behind the toilet signaling that he wanted to stand up to pee and lean spread eagle against the wall to urinate in the bowl. This would scare me because he was so rigid he might fall. Sometimes he couldn't get a stream going unless you left the bathroom; and he would signal you to leave. God save us if he ever fell off the toilet. But safety was not really his consideration; privacy while peeing was. So be it. We'd leave the door ajar ready to leap in if he teetered.

If he missed the bowl while urinating, he wanted you to wipe it up off the floor, just as he wanted you to wipe his rear end after moving his bowels. He wanted to be reassured that he was clean. He cared about the floor as much as he cared about how well you helped him. I always thought that was such a fundamental expression of dignity—even when he had lost so much of his function.

In his last five years, when it came to eating, John was a vacuum, one that had a lot of fun. Huntington's disease impairs metabolism and often people need far more calories when they are well into the progression of their disease. There were three prototypical scenarios as John became increasingly disabled. First, there was a period when he fed himself, although clumsily: hot dogs by the half-dozen, watermelons by the half-melon, milk shakes by the blender full. Asking him if he wanted more was only a ritual because he'd always say "Yup! More!" with that grin on his face—often partially obscured by a face full of chocolate ice cream. These were fun times for him. Yes, it was a mess and fatiguing to him because it was work, but, he rarely became short-tempered or impatient eating. It was fun or a game, and he loved playing it with both fellow residents and staff. There were thousands, literally, hollow leg jokes and he'd laugh anew every time.

As time went on, he needed more help and he really had to concentrate on using his increasingly rigid arms and impaired grasp to spoon food into his mouth. Of course, there were staff nearby willing to help him; but, again, John was all about doing it for himself. He actively rejected offers of assistance. In fact, sometimes, staff would take the remnants of a plate and say "Let me help you with this last bite" just to fool him into accepting a bit of help. No way. Somehow, with a glare or sometimes by being quicker with the fork, he'd make sure he even got the last forkful without help.

Finally, as the end of his long road approached, when he had to have help simply to get food into his mouth, watching him struggle was heartrending. But struggle he did. It was anguishing to watch him struggle to move a spoonful of ice cream, placed by staff into his mouth, from the front of his mouth to the back for swallowing. There was a time that his control was so impaired that his tongue would thrust outward often ejecting the food; but, he was never deterred. At this time, he was not losing weight and he was well nourished. He didn't have to have that snack or those extra calories in "Snack Club." It was in front of him, and he had a helper and plenty of time to do it. To see this effort expended with no expression of frustration or annoyance to do such a simple thing, with visible signs of fatigue to do it, was humbling.

Some of us may talk about quality of life and assess that John didn't have much of it during these times. But, if you consider the notion of a will to live and assess it by the quantum effort it takes to do the smallest things, man, John had it. It humbled all who worked with him and shared some time helping him to eat, toilet, or share a laugh.

[This shows the difference between Robert and John. Robert simply gave up.]

On rare occasions, those of us who worked 9 to 5, would come in to learn that John had caused some problems as reported by staff. Fair or unfair to that staff, we always assumed that the staff member involved had triggered the alleged misbehavior. No need for investigation; they must have blown it. That's how predictable and consistent John was. Somebody must not have been listening to him or kept him waiting an unreasonable amount of time. He didn't ask for much from the staff. Essentially, he wanted to be up for things that were happening, in bed when he was tired, taken to the bathroom, bathed, dressed, and have his TV set to cartoons (Thanks, George!) and then, years later, tuned for him to Channel 41 on weekdays at 4:30 p.m. for Chuck Norris in "Walker: Texas Ranger."

Occasionally, he would raise a ruckus, but typically it would be to go to the business office to see if he had money in his account and, preferably, a few bucks in his wallet. This could be a problem if one didn't understand him. But, simply, he would cool down just as fast as he would heat up when he couldn't make himself clear.

As impaired as his ability to communicate eventually became, these scenarios are unified in my memory as examples of how clear John was about what he wanted as well as how hard he would work to do things, no matter how difficult they became for him, and how little he'd expect people to do for him. We often talk about John being a simple man. Sometimes, we talk about it in the context of his perhaps being mildly retarded or delayed developmentally in some way. Yes, that may be true, but in addition, he was simple in a wise, more profound and spiritual way. He wanted very little for himself. He didn't want much help getting it. And he'd let you know, someway, somehow, when you were blocking his way. It's kind of a spiritual thing. And it was so simple that the fucking Huntington's could not impair this spirit in any way.

I don't want to get too heavy into this, but that's it. I think that I spent damn near the better part of fifteen years with John. My visual memories are his grin and his ice cream smeared face. My recollections are a set of funny stories, like, wearing a dress every Halloween.

But when I think of John, it's really a spirit that I think of. What a teacher he was. Wasn't he?"

I give thanks that I have been blessed to walk along side of Robert and John in their long and too short struggles. I have been taught much by these two humble and quiet men by the dignity and grace that they exhibited on their way to death's door.

Death is an evil, intemperate woman. It is something that you fear and something that you embrace. I just wish there had been a guide book to help me through it. It was mentally draining to come see the boys and visually inspect their bodies, using my fingers as lenses to my mind, as I watched their bodies slowly disintegrate. Hard decisions needed to be made regarding their medical needs as they slowly descended into the well of death. The dealings that I had in escorting my brother Robert to death's door assisted me with the slow and arduous journey as John embarked upon that path.

There were no rules or guidebooks to help make life and death decisions over someone else's life. I could have used one in making the decision to get John and Robert out of society and into the necessary nursing facilities. I had to manipulate the health care system in order to get necessary and adequate long term care and safety for both John and Robert.

After John's death on March 26, 2006, his ashes were in my home. With many months of soul searching and having John rest on my étagère, during October 2007, I finally found the best place to lay his ashes to rest. I buried them at the base of the arborvitae trees that I had planted in my back yard in John and Robert's memory. When I finally put John's ashes into the ground, I came to peace with the decisions I had made; I knew that I did the right things for both boys.

I did not want to intercede in Robert and John's lives but I had to. Who was I to make these decisions about someone else's life? I just always prayed for guidance and that I could do what was in their best interest. I feel that I have done that. Having never really known Robert and my father, I do not know what caused me to have compassion for them but I have always tried to help in any way I could. Robert and John lived on the fringe of the societal norm. They were not bad; they just didn't have the mental capacity to conduct themselves in a civilized way.

Not until I started searching court and hospital documents involving my family's history did I find out that our mother was treated for Huntington's Chorea and her mother before her, although the condition of Huntington's was not recognized at that time. My brothers and sisters knew nothing of Huntington's disease and its effect on our family until I shared with them John's diagnosis and that Huntington's is a genetic disease. My eldest sister, Kathleen, had told me that Mother had died from Muscular Dystrophy and she never knew of Huntington's. Our father always kept to himself and never discussed any family matters with his children and we dared not ask.

When I took on the responsibility of caring for John, I found out how physically and mentally destructive Huntington's disease can be. Each of us six kids had the potential to pass on this disease. Because of this and because of the abject poverty in which I grew up, I chose not to have children. It is a decision I have often regretted because I love children.

If one of your parents is a Huntington's carrier or has Huntington's disease, you have no idea whether or not you will have the disease or be a carrier unless you get genetically tested.

Finding out that you will develop the disease sometime in your life or that you are a carrier and your children have a good chance of having the disease can be devastating.

There is, however, a note of hope. When my grandmother had the disease, she was institutionalized in an insane asylum. At the time there was no treatment and no medications for Huntington's. From my mother's time to my brothers' time, many medications were developed to ameliorate their conditions, and specialized skilled nursing facilities were developed. The advancements in detecting and treating Huntington's give hope that someday the disease will be eradicated. On January 1, 2016 in New York State, there will be a new medical weapon in fighting the Huntington's disease—medical marijuana. The wild movement of arms and legs is called the Chorea, commonly referred to as The Dance. It is believed and hoped that the medical marijuana will lessen these wildly uncontrolled movements and slow down the progression of the disease.

There is one more brother. He is the oldest of us boys. That is Arthur Jack Knauer, Jr. whom I always called "Junior." In December 1982, just after his thirty-ninth birthday, he went to a small community hospital in Ellenville, New York for chest pains. He was advised that he was in need of triple bypass surgery. His girlfriend Maryann contacted me because he was refusing to have the surgery. At this point I saw a golden opportunity. I contacted him and reminded him of the haircut and making me eat the cigar many years earlier. I told him that if he didn't come with me to Albany Med, I would gladly return the favor.

On January 22 of 1983, he was admitted to Albany Medical Center for the bypass operation. It was an extremely snowy and cold winter. That morning I met with him where he was prepped with IV's and markings on his chest ready to go to the operating room. I was told that I should not come back until around five in the evening. When I got to the recovery room, they told me he was still in ICU. I went there, and the lines of patients were still waiting. He looked pretty gray. He had been bumped from surgery for more critical patients who had come in. They scheduled him for surgery the next morning. And yes, Gentlemen, you've got it. It happened all over again the next day. When I arrived that evening, he was demanding his clothes and checking himself out. It was the first time I ever saw him frightened about his condition and what had transpired. I really thought I'd have to go out to the truck, get a rope, and tie him to the bed. He knew I'd do it!

On the morning of the third day, I was there bright and early. I met with Junior and the surgeon and made reference to the doctor about the six-inch folding knife on my belt and said, "One of you two sons-of-bitches are going to come down from the operating room with a hole." Later that afternoon the surgeon called me at work and told me that the operation had been a success.

Art stayed with me for ten weeks while he recovered. I asked him to write about the experience. First thing he wrote was, "I knew from the very start living with George would not be easy. We are like oil and water."

I still had to make a living while he was recovering. He recalls the first time I left him alone:

> George said to me, 'In the meantime see what you
> can find to fix for dinner.'

I had just come from under the knife, and here he is giving orders. Damn, I hated it there already. After he left, I opened his refrigerator to find nothing but water and a few other things that had hair on it. From there I went to his food cabinets. There was a can of fish and a box of spaghetti, so I made him dinner with both. He was surprised that I could make so fine a meal with nothing, but he enjoyed every mouthful. George damn near had a heart attack when I told him he would have to let me go shopping for food if he were to go on having nice meals. He agreed, but he didn't realize what the bill was going to come to. When I tell you he had nothing, I am not kidding you. His cabinet was filled with air and that's all. So I got him to drive us to the town of Catskill to buy food. When I was done shopping, we had a full cart. The bill came to about a hundred and thirty dollars. Back then, that was a lot. He screamed at me and made all kinds of "buts," but he paid the bill and we went home. He didn't like paying out, but he sure liked the way real food tasted.

Junior had one other big complaint. The doctor said that he had to walk a mile every day, so I had to push him out the door and tell him he could not come back until he had done the mile. It really did snow a lot that year. On many occasions, the snow was coming down so hard you could not see the street. Art recalls, "No matter what, he made sure I went. The funny part of all this is that he was right there at my side, to make sure I didn't fall."

I lived in a one bedroom trailer. During these ten weeks I slept on the couch while he slept in my nice comfortable king-sized bed. Junior wrote, "George gave up a lot for me that winter: his bed and his money for I had no job and no income, but he bitched every day about having to sleep on his couch. I had a lady friend at the time, who came up to be with me. George liked her so he gave her the run of the place while she was there."

In the Good Book, Cain asks God, "Am I my brother's keeper?" I don't have to ask that question: I have been my brothers' keeper.

6. About Going Blind

Life's light does not shine through the eyes but from the heart ~

I went blind in April 2002. I strongly feel that what caused my blindness may date as far back as 1988—to my bull headedness. I had just purchased a new two-and-half-ton truck with a snow plow and a utility body. I was out at a customer's house after a wet and heavy snowfall. As I pushed the snow past the end of the driveway, the front end of the truck suddenly dropped off into a soft spot. Because of the weight on the blade in the front of the truck, I was unable to lift the blade hydraulically. I thought that if I disconnected the blade and moved it away from the truck, I could get a running start and drive the truck out from the snow drift. My truck was equipped with a two-way radio which I shared with an electrician, a well driller, and several other people. After repeatedly attempting to raise someone to come tow me out, I proceeded to get the truck deeper and deeper into the packed snow and ice. With a great deal of anger, I pushed and dragged the plow with my bare hands and moved the plow away from the truck.

Finally, Richie Kerr, the electrician, heard my call on the radio and came to help tow me out from the field. Richie realized that I had pushed and dragged the snow plow, which weighed over 1000 pounds, over 100 feet away from where the truck was. He said I was mad to do that. Later he told me that when he first saw me there he was so frightened by my demeanor that he grabbed a shovel to use as a weapon in case I was going to be violent.

When I got back home, I walked down the hall to the bathroom and passed out, hitting the floor. My wife at the time, her step-daughter, and Richie Kerr were in the living room, heard me collapse, and called the rescue squad. Manning the Rescue Squad Ambulance were Gina McGrath, her son Mark, and Mark De Francesco. They recall that I was completely irrational; it took both men, actually lying on top of me, to hold me down. They feared that I might hurt someone, or get loose and jump out of the ambulance.

When I came to in the Catskill Hospital Emergency Room, I didn't know where I was. My body was strapped to the bed and my wrists were tied to the side of the bed with three inch straps which I proceeded to break without any effort. Several people tried to restrain me in the bed—I was tossing them about as if they were toy children. My strength was amazing. It was as if I had developed super human strength. I was quite strong in my day-to-day life because I was a plumber having to lift boilers, heavy machinery such as rotor rooters, water heaters and pipes; but this particular day, I was far in excess of normal strength. Numerous times the doctor asked my friend Barry Rausch what kind of illegal drugs I had taken. (I have never taken drugs in my life.)

This incident in 1988 may or may not have been a prelude to

the difficulties that followed. After this, there were many times when I would do irrational things. I would speak to people and not remember later. My friends referred to these episodes as "crash and burns." I believe these incidents, starting with moving the snow plow, led up to my major "crash and burn" in April 2002 which resulted in a stroke, the loss of my sight, and severe nerve damage.

Between late 2000 and 2002, I was working seven days a week and going back and forth to the hospital and the nursing home to care for my two critically ill brothers who were dying of Huntington's disease. My brothers were in two different states, so this required a lot of traveling. I was on the road for six or seven hours at a time.

Thirteen months before going blind I had another "crash and burn." Sam Mento, a Coxsackie police officer, describes his encounter with me below:

> On Saturday, January 6, 2001, approximately 9:45 p.m., as an officer of the Coxsackie Police force, I was on duty and patrolling upper Mansion Street. It was a quiet night and I was running radar. Not much was happening. The [Reed's Landing] Bistro had people going in and out as you would expect on a Saturday night. I got a dispatch from state police: "You have a drunk and disorderly subject on lower Reed Street who is trying to break into cars." Naturally I fly down to Reed Street, lights, no siren, and I am scanning the sides of both sidewalks looking for my drunk disorderly subject. As I am proceeding down the street, I see a person (you) in the doorway of your building by the store front

laying against the side of the vestibule. As I approach I say, "George are you ok?" My initial thoughts are that the drunk disorderly subject may have assaulted you. You respond, "I'm looking for my horse do you see him?" I say, "George, this is Sam, are you ok?" You reply, "He's around here somewhere. I think my sword is here somewhere." Still not sure what is going on, I assume by now you were the drunk disorderly subject I got called about. You apparently were staggering and whoever called had thought you were drunk as you were falling into the parked cars before you wound up in your vestibule. Being an RN, besides a cop and knowing you, I immediately begin to think hypoglycemic, stroke, something medical, as I know you are not an abuser of spirits or substances. I help you to your feet and get you up to your apartment on the second floor and help you onto the bed. I contacted dispatch stating what the status was and that I needed an ambulance for transport as it seemed to me you were obviously dealing with a medical issue. I know you were seeing a woman at the time. I contacted her. The ambulance arrived along with your lady friend. But as we waited together, you were concerned about not being able to find your sword and horse as you had been roping horses and slaying dragons. The ambulance arrived and we all carried you down the stairs and you were taken to Albany Medical Center. This was, I believe, the beginning of something. I told Cindy about the incident and we both thought perhaps you were diabetic and this may have been just an odd incident that was easily remedied. I guess it was only the beginning as it turns out.

On February 1, 2002, I had laproscopic surgery on my left shoulder to clean out excess calcium in the shoulder joint. The doctors said that I should take the next six to ten weeks off and keep my left arm in a sling. I was self-employed, and if I didn't do work or respond to the customers' calls, they would go to the first available plumber and I would have lost that customer. I had a truck and mortgage payments and I needed to work to maintain the survival of Knauer Plumbing and Heating. So, I went to work.

Sunday, April 7, 2002 at 9:00 p.m. I received a call on my pager from Horton Hospital in Middletown, New York. My brother Robert, who was institutionalized because of his Huntington's Chorea, was in critical shape because his airway was blocked. His lower denture had fallen parallel into his throat. I was his legal and physical guardian. I immediately approved surgery and then took off from Coxsackie to Middletown as I knew Robert was "meaner than a junk yard dog" and there was going to be physical trouble between him and the staff when he came out of surgery. I arrived at the hospital around 11:15 p.m., and Security let me in the building and took me to Robert's room. When I entered the room, I saw that Robert had torn out his IV tubes. With his six foot tall, two hundred eighty pound frame, he had a nurse in each hand and blood everywhere. After he heard me bellow some definitive expletives, he lay back and let the nurses care for him. Over the next week I went there after work each night, returning to Coxsackie for two hours of sleep.

On Friday April 11, I checked Robert out of the Horton Hospital and into a full service nursing home as a temporary measure until I could get him to Laurel Lake in Lee, Massachusetts where I had previously placed our brother John who was suffering the same fate. I knew he would be properly cared for there. I was tired and overwhelmed by all that was going on in addition to working seven days a week for the past year. I knew that I was the only one of my family who would step up to the plate and take care of him.

On Friday, April 12, I was working at Mary's Pine Hollow Camp Ground. I was using a six foot ice bar, poking the ground in an attempt to find seven septic tanks in order to put in concrete rings raising them above grade level so that the tanks could be pumped that afternoon and the state inspector could look at them on Monday. I had to get the job done. The more I used the ice bar to probe the ground, the worse the pain got. My left shoulder was absolutely on fire. Death would have been less painful, but I let my mind overrule the pain and continued until I completed the job.

For some reason, I have always been able to disregard pain and discomfort. I could just turn that sensation off in my head and do what I had to do. Once when I had third degree burns on my wrist from picking up a boiler I had just cut up with a torch, I didn't feel it. When my friend Gina McGrath noticed it the next day, she made sure I went to the doctor. It wasn't the severity of the burn that bothered the doctor but the fact that I did not know that I had burned my wrist. This is only one example.

I believe that as I continued to use the ice bar that Friday before I went blind, I was aggravating the poisoning in my shoulder starting an irreversible chain of tragedy that led to my near death and eventual blindness.

On the next day, Saturday, April 13, I helped a friend move

from Athens, New York to Hudson, New York. The sky became ominous as if it was going to pour any minute and I had all of her possessions in the back of my pickup truck, so I did not dawdle. I moved quickly up and down the stairs, working up a sweat and getting an uneasy feeling throughout my body.

When I arrived home, my friend Ricky Cure showed up with his BMW motorcycle and asked if I wanted to go for a ride. I asked him when he was going to get a real bike, a Harley, instead of that sewing machine on wheels. He did not have to ask twice for me to get my new 2002 Harley Dyno Low Rider motorcycle out. The Harley was my dream. I had everything chromed that could be chromed, and it rode sweeter than anything you could dream of. My Harley was my mistress. I had worked a lifetime to get her. We rode down to Hager's Harbor, a little bar in Athens, New York, for a quick couple of beers. As we came back to Coxsackie, Ricky went in one direction and I in another to go home. Somewhere around this time, I must have begun losing contact with reality because I later found out that I had left my $25,000 sweetheart Harley parked outside with the keys in the ignition and my helmet hanging on the handle bars. Little did I realize that that would be my final ride on this beauty, having put only 150.4 miles on her.

After returning home from riding my Harley with Ricky, my body was going into the beginning stages of shutting down. I recently remembered that I was sitting at the counter having a drink of orange juice and eating grapes when suddenly my right eye went blank—I could not see with it. I rubbed my eyes and said to myself, "I'm so damn tired I think I will go lay down." That was the start of losing my sight.

Later that week, when I was in ICU, a friend found my Harley outside with the keys in the ignition and the helmet hanging from the handle bars. She called her son-in-law, Dave, who put the bike inside my building. She took the keys and put them in the leather jacket pocket, and then put both the helmet and jacket upstairs in the front closet. I never would have left my precious Harley like this if something weren't wrong with me at the time.

In the wee hours of April 14, I got up to go to the bathroom. I passed out and collapsed onto the floor. When I regained consciousness, I must have called Mark Evans, Gina McGrath's older son who had extensive medical training, and told him what had happened. He called the Rescue Squad. The only memory I have from then on is of the rescue squad captain, a certified EMT, kneeling over me and saying to Mark Evans that he was not getting a pulse. Mark replied, "I think I have a faint one."

The Coxsackie Rescue Squad drove me to the New York Thruway where the Albany Paramedic Ambulance Advance Life Support team got on board and proceeded from there to Albany Medical Center, a Trauma One facility. Because I have no memory of this, I asked my dear friend Gina to fill me in. She wrote:

On Sunday, April 14, 2002, the lives of George Knauer and those who loved him changed forever. After church, I came downtown just by chance and saw the Rescue Squad at George's apartment building. As I ran over, Bob Frank yelled to me to get upstairs, something had happened to George. (That was the fastest that I ever climbed those stairs.) As I entered his bedroom, I saw my son Mark taking George's vital signs. I asked George what happened and he was able to tell me that he had awakened during the night and passed out on his way to the bathroom. After coming to, he returned to bed thinking this would pass with more sleep. However, around 10:00 am it happened again. After once again getting to his bed, he called Mark and told him he needed help. Mark rushed down and the Rescue Squad was called. I asked George if he had any pain, thinking perhaps he had a head injury from falling. At this point, he was still able to talk and give appropriate answers.

Mark relayed his concern with George's extremely low blood pressure and as the ambulance was leaving, I called George's sister Rosemary who lives in Pennsylvania, three hours away, to let her know we were on our way to Albany Medical Center Hospital and I would let her know what was happening.

Upon arriving at Albany Medical Center Hospital, the crew told me that George was having increased difficulty breathing and was less responsive. He was immediately put into Trauma One, so I knew that while he would receive good care, this was not a good sign. Doctors and nurses hurried to take care of him, all the time asking me questions about his medical history and habits. George was having more and more difficulty breathing and tried to sit up to get his breath although he was not really able to respond to the doctors' and nurses' questions and directions. George was sedated and the decision was made to intubate him; it was a difficult intubation, but successful after several tries. The doctors then attempted to rule out certain things—namely an aortic aneurysm. A cardio-thoracic surgeon was called in and tests done right in the room as he was deemed too critical to move; those tests came back negative. Later at the hospital, the doctors told us that if he had not called Mark, he would not have lasted through the afternoon.

His pressure continued to plummet although he was being infused at a wide open rate. One doctor asked about relatives and I told him that George had a sister in Pennsylvania. He asked how long it would take for her to get to the hospital. When I told him, three to four hours, he said, "Call her immediately. He may not be with us by that time." I called Rosemary. She and her husband Guy Allen left as soon as they got off the phone. I also contacted Artie (George's oldest brother) and Barry (a friend who was visiting in Lake George). The staff gave us a special room reserved for families of critical patients and we remained there for many hours. Rosemary and Guy arrived and I was certainly glad to have company! We were allowed to be with George as much as we wanted and looked for every small sign that he might survive. One time, we took a break and went to get something to eat. Upon returning about twenty minutes later, we found that his blood pressure had not gone down any further and noted that to the nurse in the room who told us not to get our hopes up too high. Rosemary answered that we would take even little miracles. In an effort to figure out what was happening, one of my sons went to George's home and brought all of his medicines to the hospital for the doctors to look at.

George had arrived at the hospital at about 11:30 a.m. Thirteen hours later, he had been infused with thirteen liters (nine liters is usually the maximum) and his body was swollen almost beyond recognition. We were told we could stay in the room but not to touch him because he could start bleeding anywhere almost immediately. Cotton was put in between his fingers to keep his bloated body from touching and causing bleeding. The pink tears coming from his eyes were the blood vessels rupturing.

His core body temperature had risen so high that the oxygen line literally melted and crystallized into the back of his neck, leaving a permanent scar. His blood pressure had "stabilized" at somewhere near 65/35 and the decision was made to take him to ICU. He was then in a medically induced coma. After accompanying him to ICU, Rosemary, Guy, and I left. Upon arriving at George's home, Rosemary and Guy realized they had left home with no clothes, no toothbrushes etc. Thank goodness George always has extras of everything. All of us were so tired, more emotionally than physically, and tried to get some rest.

Thank God that Gina was there because she knew more of my medical history than I cared to remember and knew how to contact my family. Also, most of what I know about the initial stages of this disaster was relayed to me by my sister and Gina.

Arthur could not be bothered to come that day because he was having a new door installed, but he reluctantly showed up the next day. He immediately got confrontational with Rosemary over my property, assets, will, and where all the pertinent paper work was. To quote my sister, she told him, "Go fuck yourself." Arthur left and never returned. I did not see Arthur until two and half years later. My other sister Kathleen never came at all. She never sent a card or called. This was a great disappointment to me.

The hospital worked very hard to save my life. In the initial hours after my arrival, because of my unintentional violent and combative state due to severe pain and trying to breathe, they put me in an induced coma in order to proceed with testing.

Because they had ruled out everything else, the doctors began to suspect some type of infection. Gina recalls that that evening the two doctors came and checked for fluid in my shoulder because I had recently had laparoscopic surgery on my shoulder and I had spent the past week working on several plugged-sewer jobs. They drew fluids and in twenty-four to forty-eight hours they would know the type of infection. They tested several cuts and bruises elsewhere, as well. They still didn't know what the problem was but suspected it was an infection throughout my entire body. The conclusion that they finally reached was that I was suffering from a combination of septicemia and hyperglycemia (blood poisoning and very high blood sugar.)

The next day, my first day in ICU, the doctors telephoned

Rosemary at eight o'clock the next morning. They wanted to try an experimental medication and she would have to sign off for them to proceed. Even though the doctors told her that it could kill me or might save me, she did not hesitate for one minute. There were no guarantees. Either way, there was not much difference, for without the medication I would die. She chose the experimental medication which turned out to save my life. By the time Rosemary got to the hospital, around 10:00 am, they had already started the first in the series of injections into my IV. Within twenty-four to forty-eight hours my kidneys and other organs started to respond.

On Tuesday, April 16, 2002, my fifty-third birthday, my family and friends told me that I looked much better. The leg bags for circulation were taken off. My feet were still swollen and my hands were still restricted with IV tubes. I had two tubes in my throat, an oxygen tube and a feeding tube. The heart specialist, Dr. Philip came and said there was no heart problem but all the organs could be affected later. They started weaning me off the medicines to see if my vital organs could hold their own.

After the third day, the multitude of doctors was replaced by one doctor who explained what tests they were doing, what they believed was happening, and what the next steps would be. They advised my sister to make funeral arrangements. She turned and told the doctor, "He is too stupid and too stubborn to die."

On the morning of the sixth day of being in a coma, I regained partial consciousness—enough to rip out the intubation tube. I saw blood all over my shirt and sheets. The nurses came running into the room. I felt no pain or emotion. It was a surreal moment; I heard no sound. As I recall, it was like watching a silent movie. The very last thing I saw, with my own functioning eyes, was the nurses. That split second is frozen in my mind. They appeared in a kaleidoscope of colors, and then I went back into a coma. The doctors decided not to re-intubate me.

When I came out of the coma the second time, a friend stopped by on her way to church and I was awake in a private room. She had pictures to show me of my last septic system job at her house, but I could not see them. They tried for me to see other things, and when I could not, they called the doctors. When I told the lady doctor that I could not see, she said, "You are staring right at me." I felt no panic or anger. While everyone on the other side of my darkness seemed to go crazy, I felt calm and peaceful.

They brought me down to the ophthalmologist. He sat me in the chair and did the eye exam. As I was looking through the phoropter refractor, he remarked to whomever was in the room that I was the first case he had ever had where he would not get an answer "A" or "B" to his questions about which lens helped me to see better. After further examination, he told me bluntly, "You will be blind for life."

I was not angry over my blindness nor did I blame others. I just thought about the situation I was in. I thought about how I could survive and what I would become. The medical staff, including psychologists and psychiatrists, were very concerned about my indifference to the fact that I was blind. I see, now that I have undergone professional counseling, that I had since childhood developed a self-defense mechanism, an emotional impervious coat of armor, a sword and shield. To others this often appeared to be indifference.

Gina recalls that the doctors wanted to put me on a short course of steroids to see if it might affect any inflammation near the optic nerve and possibly help me regain some sight. They told us that it was worth a chance but that the side effects could be quite unpleasant. Were they ever right!!! During this time, I had a series of hallucinations. One time I was trying to save the "machine people." It was a dark factory full of machines that had human heads. They were dying from the lack of power. I was suspended high above the machine people. I tried helping them get up and running. I was hundreds of feet above them and screamed to them, "You can get started. You can do it!!! Come on, come on." That was pretty funny actually. There were restraints in the room and I thought I could repel down using the straps and help them. Gina tied the restraints and bell cord around me (as I directed) and the other end around herself. As she called out, "I'm going down, I'm going down," I realized that she was still standing by my side. I told her, "No, you are not; you are still here." At that point, Gina then lay down on the floor, partially under the bed to make it sound like she had repelled down to the machine people. Just then a nurse came into the room, took one look and demanded, "What is going on here?" Gina responded innocently, "We're repelling!" The nurse did not think any of this was funny and immediately went over and untied me. There were times that the hospital personnel really wondered about how my family and friends were taking care of me. Both Gina and Rosemary were wonderful at role playing and keeping me calm while trying to pull me back to reality.

Gina remembers Rosemary breaking down only once. She was afraid that I would continue to be irrational. It was very hard for my sister to see my behavior. They had to move the other patient out of the room and have someone sit with me all the time behind closed doors. While I was in the ICU ward, there were many times that my mind told me that I was anywhere but there. At times, I was convinced that I had driven my truck into the hospital and that the truck was my hospital bed. Other times I thought that my bed was two-thirds a Lincoln car and one-third hospital bed. In my drug-induced state, I thought I was parked in town or a public parking lot. When I was told that friends were coming to see me, I would ask, "Don't you think we should get back to the hospital?" Another time, I had to go to the bathroom. Believing that I was living in Rosemary's basement, I saw a floor drain, and, without hesitation, I leaned over the side of the bed to relieve my bladder. Unfortunately, I was urinating on some equipment in the ICU ward. Whenever I rang for the bedpan after that, it amazed me that the nurses could find me wherever I imagined I was. Many times I thought I was being held captive. I believed that I was going to break free from my captors (nurses). In reality, I was trying to climb out of bed, remove my IV, and doing unintentional harm to myself.

Another time, I was held underground in a secret basement room by the nurses where they were doing experiments on me. I swiped a spoon from the food tray, and when they weren't looking, I used the spoon to try to tunnel out and crawl up through the wall and across the ceiling to get away from them. On another occasion, I thought I heard water leaking in a toilet. I told Rosemary to get my plumbing tools. I wanted to fix the toilet in order to save the home owner money. Actually I was hearing the IV drip.

As I came out of the coma, the doctors' wrote in my chart that "notably the patient has a striking indifference to his acute blindness." A psych consult was ordered to investigate the possibility of a conversion disorder (meaning that my blindness could be psychosomatic), although they thought this unlikely because both ophthalmology and neuro-opthalomology doctors had examined me when my blindness first became apparent and reported that the blindness seemed real because I had no pupilary reflex.

The seeming indifference I displayed was due to the fact that I had more important things to focus on. Within five days after coming out of the coma, I realized that I had to immediately resume caring for my brothers, Robert and John, who suffered from Huntington's Chorea. There was no one else willing to take on the task. I phoned Jim Pollard, the director of the Huntington's disease program at Laurel Lake. I advised him to go ahead with the transfer necessary to have my brother Robert moved from Middletown, New York to Lee, Massachusetts. Robert entered the nursing home on May 1of 2002. Maybe if I had walked away twenty years ago from taking care of John and Robert, I would still have my sight and would still be working as a plumber, running my own business. Even knowing what I know now, I would do it all again. In retrospect, waking up blind but having the responsibility of my brothers' lives in my hands forced me to concentrate on reality.

When I first was able to have visitors, about eight or ten friends came to my bed side. Their love and support was overwhelming— as were their voices to my ears. The voices were like the roar of a thousand trains. It took me several years to learn to filter sound.

A friend, Dave Merchant, came to my bedside. He asked me what I was going to do for a living now that I was blind. Without missing a beat, I said: "I am going to start a whore house. I can still taste, test, and feel the goods." Within days, my buddy Dave had half of Coxsackie knowing what my future occupation was going to be.

There were many friends that came to my hospital bedside. Among the first were Vicki Ecker, Dave Merchant, Diane Ringwald,

Claudia Labuda, Tim Albright, and Peggy Quigley. Scott Purdy, Elder of the Twelve Tribes (a religious order from Coxsackie), and Louis Betke (the Sewer Superintendent) came numerous times to visit.

During one visit, I imagined that I was floating through the window, higher and higher above the hospital. I hate heights. The higher I rose, the louder I screamed and the more I struggled. Louis and my brother-in-law held me down on the bed with their hands trying to convince me that I was down and safe. In my mind, I was anywhere but down and safe.

There were many of these delusional activities over the three month period. Many times in my delusion I could talk to those around me but my visual surroundings were not representative of where I really was in a hospital room.

The medical staff asked questions to see what possible memory loss I incurred. For example, they asked who the President was, and I surprised them by giving his full name, George Walker Bush. I had no idea, however, what the date was as I had no conception of how long I had been in the hospital. In many ways, I had lost touch with reality. One time when they did a biopsy of my optic nerve, I thought that I was in an old mansion, in the center of a forest of beautiful cherry blossom trees.

One of my dear friends, my pal, leaned over and whispered in my ear, "Don't worry about your building. You will not lose your home." I had not thought about my home, but with my friend's words I realized I had to think about my economic future. These words, even heard in my psychotic and delusional state, took a great weight off of my mind. When I finally came home and started mobility and rehabilitation training, one of the officers from The

National Bank of Coxsackie, on Reed Street, came to me and also indicated that my building was secure and not to worry about losing it.

On one occasion my family brought some documents for me to sign. Among the papers was a For Sale sign intended for one of my trucks. The next morning it mysteriously appeared over my bed. It was decided, that I would go to the highest bidder. The sign followed me as I was moved from room to room. About a week before my discharge, a nurse offered $12.95 if the bed were included. The amusement we all got from this helped to alleviate the boredom and frustration of long days. Some doctors and nurses noticed the sign and laughed along with us. Others were not amused, and still others felt the need to stick up for me!

I remember that on May 5, for the first time after weeks of being in the hospital, Gina was allowed to take me outside in a wheel chair to the parking lot. The sounds of cars, buses, and people were deafening. The sun and the strong winds on my face hurt. I felt as if I were getting burned. It was then I realized that I would always need glasses and a hat to shade my eyes from the sun and wind. Out of nowhere, I heard a motorcycle. I turned to Gina and said, "That's Pat and Charlie." She was shocked when she realized I was right. I asked them what they were doing in Albany. They told me, "Today is our twenty-ninth wedding anniversary and who better to spend it with than you? It was you who introduced us." They stayed about ten minutes, and I could not wait to get away from all of the sounds. After they left, Gina and I went to the cafeteria and got some ice cream for a treat.

When I was strong enough to stand, my sister Rosemary took me out into the hallway so that I could get some exercise. She went to the far end of the hall and talked to me. In lieu of a cane, the maintenance man cut me a broom handle about fifty-eight inches long. There were beds, chairs, night tables, and oxygen tanks all along the hall. We would practice with me using the "cane" to get around these obstacles and I would eventually reach her by following her voice. We did this many times; sometimes the doctors and nurses thought that Rosemary was too harsh in making me walk the gauntlet. I felt that she made it way too easy.

I had been bedridden for the better part of a month. The doctors had used pneumatic socks on my legs, but still I developed a six inch blood clot in my left calf. I waited five days for the surgeon to cut the blood clot out of my leg. When he came, he told me that I would lose all feeling to my left foot. At that point, I asked him, "What are you, fucking crazy? I am blind and you want to take away another sense. How would I know if I am walking off a curb or feel what is beneath my foot?" An hour after I told the doctor he was crazy, I was discharged. That was on May 7.

I had gone into the hospital weighing two hundred-fourteen pounds (muscle not fat) and came home weighing one hundred-seventy four pounds. The first place I went was to Richie Bruno's Barber Shop. I didn't need a haircut, I needed shearing. When I went to pay, he wouldn't take my money. Next we proceeded to Sbarboro's, where I ordered a big, juicy, greasy hamburger with french fries covered with gravy. Rosemary, Guy and Gina enjoyed the same. After eating hospital food for the length of my stay, this was a gourmet's delight. When we went to pay, the lunch bill was taken care of by the owner, Lynn Brockett, to welcome me back. Over the last fourteen years of being blind, she and her employees have been caring and supportive. Sbarboro's is the

Cheers of restaurants—"where everyone knows your name." I was overwhelmed by the number of people that came over to the table to say that they were glad that I was home. Michael from the local funeral parlor was the first to say welcome home and I replied, "I hope you don't mind that I cheated you out of a job." After lunch, we went across the street to my home to find the Twelve Tribes (a local religious group) just finishing installing the banister rails along my staircase. They also would not accept payment for their services. I lived on the second floor of my building and attempted to go up my stairs. My good friend Barry Rausch grabbed my belt and all but carried me up the stairs to my bed. I had absolutely no strength. Over the following years, I would have lost my building if it had not been for his repairing the outside electrical distribution systems, wiring my new apartment on the third floor and coming to assist when I have had medical emergencies.

While I was in the hospital, I had received as many as two hundred get well cards. Rosemary and Gina posted the cards all over the wall. When I left the hospital, I insisted that the cards come with me and be put in the hallway of my home so my friends could see them as they came into visit.

Soon after I came home, there was a party for me at the Quarry Steak House where over five hundred people came to welcome me home.

When I came home, I was in unbearable pain. The medication that I was taking did not reduce the level of discomfort. Finally on May 14, I was overwhelmed by the pain. My sister insisted that I go back to the hospital. I remained at the hospital until May 16 while they did a series of tests. The tests were inconclusive and the pain in my left temple still occurs occasionally to this day.

Shortly after I got home the second time, Gina took me down to the Greene County Medical Arts building where I had a follow up ultra-sound of the blood clot. After the test, I sat up and put my shoes and socks back on. When I started to stand up, the technician said, "Where the hell do you think you are going? You may have walked in here, but you are going to leave here in a wheel chair. You sure the hell are not going to die in here. If you want to die, go outside." That was the first time I was told how potentially deadly the blood clot was.

In the following days, the Greene County visiting nurse would come to my home to draw bloods and take my blood pressure each day. Part of my medical routine was getting injections of Coumadin in my stomach around the belly button to help dissolve the clot, plus about twenty-seven different medications for pain, depression, sleep, blood pressure, and diabetes.

On May 22, the Commission for the Blind came to my home to evaluate my condition and assess my need for mobility train-ing, assistance with independent living at home, and computer instructions. The Commission for the Blind subcontracts all of the necessary training for independent living and home skills to the Northeast Association for the Blind of Albany.

On Friday of that week, while the visiting nurse was here drawing my bloods and checking my vitals, she became alarmed and called my local physician. She thought that I should be rushed to Albany Medical Center immediately. Based on what she had told him, he thought that it was not urgent and could wait for Monday. I had told no one that I was having terrible chest pains and shortness of breath. While I knew that something was wrong, I was determined that I would not go anywhere until I signed a will and left DNR orders. That could not be done until first thing on Monday morning. I wanted everything taken care of so that there would not be a repeat of what happened on April 15, with family members squabbling over who was in charge and who was to take over control of my business and personal assets.

After I signed my legal documents, I allowed my sister and Gina to take me to the physician's office on May 28. When I arrived, the nurse and doctor rushed to get me hooked up to four different machines. They called for an ambulance to take me to Albany Medical Center.

The blood clot had broken free from my ankle and gone to my lungs. When I returned to the hospital on Tuesday, I was extremely distraught and screaming. I did not want to be there. The last time I was there I lost my sight, had a series of TIA's (small strokes), suffered excruciating pain in my left leg from nerve damage and a dislocated knee cap, and the doctor wanted to cut the blood clot from my calf leaving my foot numb. Now back in the ER, another doctor wanted to put a filter in my chest wall to keep the clot from breaking off and going to my heart or brain and killing me instantly. They call this filter a "Christmas tree filter." I asked the doctor what were the percentages that the filter would work and if it would ever have to be replaced. He said, "They work about sixty-five percent of the time." I told him I was a plumber for thirty-five years and any time you put a filter in a pipe it will always plug up and need replacing. I asked him how it would be installed. He said that they would use a long needle and pull it up through the artery going to my heart. Then my question was how it would be replaced. He said they would remove it from my chest surgically. I told him, "No thanks." He warned me if that blood clot broke free I would die. This doctor understood what I was saying and made me comfortable by respecting my choice. I gave the doctor my business card and told him that if he ever had any plumbing questions to call me. I was released on June 11. Within the year, he called me regarding a plumbing question he had. His gas water heater would not stay running. It would start and stop repeatedly. I asked him to describe what the unit looked like. He told me there was an exhaust blower on the top. I asked him if he had any medical tape. His answer was, "Of course." I told him to cover the back flow damper and let me know how it works out. He called me two days later. The water heater was working fine. I was more than happy to be of service.

My sister Rosemary stayed with me, helping in any way she could. One night while Rosemary was sleeping on the couch, I got up to go to the bathroom. The nerve pain in my leg and left knee was acting up, and as I hobbled, there were two huge pops in my left knee cap. The knee cap had shifted and the noise was so loud that it woke her up. The left knee is something I still have trouble with today.

Rosemary is a very good cook and slowly started to put some meat back on my bones. Not only did she make meals for me while she was here, but she also made a large pot of her beef stew and froze about a dozen containers of it. After she left, I often would sit in my recliner and eat pretzels because I was afraid to go near the stove or kitchen. One day, when she called and asked if I had been eating, I told her, "Pretzels," and she chastised me. She told me to go to the refrigerator and take out a plastic container from the freezer, let it thaw out, and eventually nuke it. I complied with my sister's instructions and went to the freezer. There were many plastic containers. I took one out and put it in the sink to allow it to thaw. About an hour later, I put it in the microwave and nuked it with great anticipation of having some of her fine stew and getting off my diet of pretzels. Finally, as the microwave started to beep, I went to the kitchen, removed the container and opened the lid, only to be shocked and dismayed. What I had thawed out and nuked, turned out to be a container of sherbet ice cream. To this day, I am still hesitant to remove anything from the freezer and nuke it.

On June 19, 2002, The Northeast Association for the Blind of Albany sent Christina Kendall, a rehabilitation specialist, to evaluate what I wanted and needed to learn and to discuss my long term goals. During this meeting, my sister, who had spent the last sixty-four days caring for me, realized that I was in good hands and went home. Christina taught me how to do daily living chores, while Ann Gallagher, a social worker, checked on my mental state.

In the following days, when I was alone, the high speed train of reality hit me. I was freefalling. I felt I was in a box of ice and I couldn't get a grip on anything to pull myself out. I couldn't get to the bathroom; I was not able to get my own food. I was disoriented, not knowing up from down or in what direction I was moving. No longer would I be able to do plumbing and heating. I didn't know how I was going to fulfill my obligations to my brothers, Robert and John, who were in a nursing home dying of Huntington's disease. I didn't know how I was going to function in the future. I was in a blackened prison. The full weight of what had happened over the past sixty-plus days had not really registered. I finally realized how deep my psychological and emotional hole was.

I recently asked Christina to share what she recalls about my mental and emotional state at this time. This is what she wrote:

When I first met George, I felt that he was a motivated and positive person who was going to make the most out of his new situation. My experience had taught me, however, that when someone first becomes blind and quickly thereafter moves into a rehabilitation program they are still usually in a state of denial about their blindness. Many people at this stage still think somewhere in their mind that their blindness is temporary and that their vision will somehow be restored. Rehab is therefore quite successful in the beginning, but as time goes on the person often slips into a depression when their vision does not come back and learning to become an independent person who is permanently blind becomes a frightening reality. Rehab programs often become delayed as the depressed person begins to cancel appointments or starts turning each daily living lesson into a counseling session. So, as I began to work with George, I waited for the crash.

Several months into his program George began to show some signs of crashing. During one lesson, George began to cry about being blind. He wondered how he would ever find work or what kind of woman would want him. Being alone, without female companionship seemed to be one of George's greatest concerns. Aloneness, of course was an understandable fear, especially coming from someone who, pre-blindness, had rarely been without a date!

Although George continued to do well with learning adaptive tasks, he spent more and more time discussing his health problems, which were somewhat alarming. George was sometimes forgetting things we had already discussed and he appeared to have mini-stroke type episodes in between our sessions where speech was slurred, etc. His friends confirmed these episodes to me and everyone was quite worried about him. More often, when he practiced his typing skills, George would describe on paper a bleak world of darkness and fear. All of this seemed normal to me considering how much George had lost in the past months and how his life had changed so dramatically. Although he described feeling like he wanted to "end it all" he also admitted that he never really felt he could go through with it. He described a local suicide that had happened the night before one of our lessons and he seemed incredulous that anyone would actually go through the act. Still, I worried somewhat that he might do something impulsive. Fortunately, that never happened.

Despite his turmoil, George continued to keep most of his lessons scheduled as well and continued to seek medical treatments for his "episodes" and caring for his two very ill brothers in nursing homes. There was so much on George's plate that he seemed to barely have enough time to think about himself.

As time wore on, and these other areas gradually cleared up, I figured George would deal more with his own emotions and discuss his fears of being blind in greater depth. This never really happened either. He did acknowledge that his blindness was probably permanent, but he rarely seemed to have an emotional connection with it. George really just described it as a factual event that couldn't be controlled or helped at that time. George always found some kind of outlet or experience in which to immerse himself. He had a new girlfriend named Anne and had also started renovating an apartment in his building. Both situations brought him great pleasure and enthusiasm. Again, I often wondered if it all was some kind of denial process or distraction, but I couldn't help but be happy for him and for him to be having positive experiences instead of just dealing with his own and his brothers' medical issues.

Now, having known George for almost seven years, I realize that George is just not someone who dwells on things that can't be changed and continues to look to the future. He was smart enough to take advantage of a few years of counseling through NABA and I believe continues with a psychologist both of which have probably helped with numerous inner issues along the way. I think it's important to note that although George is generally someone who prefers to take care of business on his own, he is not too proud to seek out professional help when needed.

George often told me that he never felt he went through all of the various stages of trauma. I always waited for it to happen but I can't really say I witnessed prolonged depression or anxiety with him. Maybe this isn't considered normal, but perhaps that's just the way it happened with George. Perhaps George's emotional outlet is channeled through constant activity and involvement with others. I think that is probably who he always was before his blindness and will probably be who he is for the rest of his life. Regardless of what it is, I believe he is a genuine example of a survivor, a fighter, and a positive spirit willing to help those in need and always ready to move on to the next chapter in his life. Although, George could best describe how his blindness has changed him as an individual, I suspect that he has never let it rob him of the essence of who he has always been. People can let trauma wreck and ruin them and I commend George for not letting it do that to him. I wish him all the luck and love in the world.

Ann Gallagher, a social worker for the Northeast Association for the Blind at Albany, was sent to assess my mental condition while Christina was helping with my physical adjustments. Ann has shared some of what she wrote in her report. On her first visit on June 27, she wrote, "Client presented as very upbeat and expressed that he was not 'depressed' or 'angry' about what had happened to him. Rather, he felt it was 'just a bump in the road' and he would have no problem recovering from the impact the loss of his vision had on him." She was concerned that I was in major denial about my situation. The next time she visited, she noted that I was tearful and very negative and hopeless about my whole situation. Obviously, I had drastic ups and downs. From the beginning of my relationship with Ann and Christina until their services were discontinued, whenever they asked questions, I answered very truthfully. I always gave an honest and full accounting.

After Rosemary went home to Pennsylvania, Gina would come by and lay out my medications, prepare my food, pay bills, keep me company, and give me shots in my stomach to help break up the blood clot that had gone to my lung. I was glad that she was there, but I often felt that she got too much joy in sticking me with the needles. I really appreciated her spending the time with me. She left her family business, a local telephone company in order to be of whatever help she could and to help my sister during this time. My sister and Gina were morally and physically supportive of each other in their care for me.

The following Monday, June 24, Gina had to return to work. She left out extra water and medication in case I needed them while she was away. I started calling my sister that night and for the subsequent five nights, begging her to send me a cocktail of medicine to terminate my life. I was in terrible pain and not thinking clearly. Obviously, she never complied with my request. I had to "suck it up" and get on with it. I put my sister Rosemary through hell, and for that, I will forever be sorry.

Meantime, On June 30, God gave me a swift kick in the ass. It was in the wee hours of that Saturday as I made my way into the bathroom that I noticed my feet were getting wet. Where was that water coming from? I thought the toilet was overflowing. I dropped to the floor and crawled over to the toilet. Using my fingers to "see," I found that one of the tank-to-bowl bolts had rusted away and water was pouring out. I turned off the water to the toilet and then grabbed every towel I owned to cover the wet floor. I was furious. Who could I get at one a.m. to fix this leaking toilet? By now, I was in excruciating pain. Here I was, a plumber, trying to figure out who could help me with a leaking toilet, and the irony of it infuriated me. I decided that I was going to fix the damn thing myself. I got to my feet, gathered all the wet towels up off the floor, and for the first time, put them in the washing machine. Then, ever so slowly, I made it over to my desk, hunting for the keys to my service truck. By holding on to the railing and using different pieces of furniture, I hobbled to the back door. As I reached for the door knob, I was scared to death. What was I doing or thinking? I realized that this was my first time going outside without someone with me. Here I was, grabbing the doorknob wearing only my slippers and tidy-whiteys. My anger kept pushing me to where I made my way out the back door and onto the back porch.

I had not yet learned to use my auditory and other senses to tell directions. I inched along with my arms out stretched and swinging wildly, hoping to find the railing and not fall down the stairs. I found the railing. It occurred to me that here was an opportunity to kill myself. I could easily have jumped over the railing. As I held onto the railing, I said to myself, "I am not that crazy. I'll be dammed if I am going to lose all of what I worked a lifetime for. Fuck that." Ever so slowly, I inched my way to the steps. Then, one cautious fearful step at a time, sliding my feet forward to the edge of each step, I went down the stairs. When I got to the last step, I thought, "Oh, God, what now?" I used the truck's electronic door lock opener on my key ring to repeatedly open and close the locks. The sound of the locks clicking told me which way and how far to go to find it. I kept moving, step by painful step, and groping with my hands out in front of me, in a newly black world for what seemed like an hour. I finally made it to my truck and climbed inside. Opening the side service doors, I had to turn around, sit down, and then pull myself into the truck. Knowing where everything was, like the back of my hand, I found the tank-to-bolt repair kit, the hacksaw and then my toolbox. Sliding out of the truck, as I tried to pick up the tools and equipment I let out a blood-curdling scream. The pain in my leg said, "Hey, Stupid, this tool box weighs twenty pounds." As I rested against the truck, my thought was, "Okay, you are here, now how do you get back?" I put the tools and myself on the ground and blindly, not certain which direction to crawl, I inched my way in what I thought was the right direction. Crawling across the black top was tearing the hell out of my skin. I made it to the back of the building. It took me forever to find my way. My first attempt put me too far to the left of the steps. Correcting my direction, I found the steps. Being in terrible pain, I rested and cried. I don't remember how long I lay there for I had fallen asleep. Once I came around and remembered where in the hell I was, I inched myself one step at a time up the two flights of stairs and lifted my tools each step ahead of me. I don't know how long I was outside or how long it took for me to get back inside, but my fury over the leaking toilet spurred me on. I cut the bolts from the toilet tank with a hack saw, installed the new bolts, replaced the ball cock and flapper, and remounted the tank to the toilet. Once I had turned the water back on and pushed the tools out of the way, I used that toilet—sitting there like a king on his throne, smiling over what I had accomplished. It took me a good amount of time. It was a milestone in my recovery. Doing the repair gave me confidence. I still had the skill, just not the sight. Then I took my first unassisted and unsupervised shower and made my way back into bed. I went to sleep knowing that I was going to live and that, for the first time in many months, I had gotten my head out of my ass and the pity party was over. After fixing that toilet, I never thought of killing myself again. Thank you, God.

I was taking 100 mg. of fentynol, 15 mg. of morphine, and two Ambien pills. On July 7, my leg was in so much pain that Gina left two extra morphine tablets. When I did not get any relief with the first pill, I took another, then another in an effort to kill the pain in my left leg.

In a state of delirium and over-medicated, I grabbed my four foot steel Viking sword in an attempt to fight off death. (Not everyone has a sword handy, but I had this particular sword hanging on my wall. It was a gift from a customer. I had been known as "The White Knight" because of my white van and ability to rescue customers from their plumbing dragons.) I remember screaming at Death, "Come on, you son-of-a-bitch, you want me, take me!" Swinging wildly, I managed to damage the wall and break some glass in a picture frame. That is when I retreated to the bedroom closet, held my sword in front of me, point down, so that it made a cross. I don't remember doing any of this, but that was where I was found later in the day, curled up in the closet hiding with my sword. Some people believed that I had tried to commit suicide over my blindness, but that was the furthest thing from the truth. I just wanted to stop the agonizing pain.

After Gina found me and was able to get me back to bed, she called my friend Barry Rausch. I do not have a clear memory of the situation, but Gina told me what occurred. Gina and Barry thought that I should go back to Albany Medical Center because of the severity of the pain. Mr. Rausch, Fire Chief, contacted the Rescue Squad Captain. They sent out an ambulance. The driver was told to go without any lights or sirens and to go to the back of my building to avoid public curiosity about what was going on. They quietly carried me down the two flights of steps.

When I was about to be discharged from the hospital on the morning of July 11, the attending physician and the hospital psychiatrist suggested that I check myself into the inpatient psychiatric unit for treatment because over the previous three months I had told doctors, family members, therapists, and several others that they "should have let me die." I agreed to this, feeling it would be helpful. The option was that, under New York State regulations, I would be held involuntarily for a mandatory seventy-two hours for psychiatric evaluation.

Once in the psychiatric unit, I was taken to a single room and asked by a young male nurse to remove my pajamas. I told him, "No way in Hell. It is freezing in this room." With that, Mrs. Cynthia Stone, a nurse, told the aide that she would take care of me. She knew me from Coxsackie for many years and made me feel safe and comfortable. I was taken to a warmer room, stripped, and photographed. This was done, I believe, to show there were no bruises or abrasions on me going into the ward.

I was very frightened. Some of the other patients were constantly screaming, some tried to steal my cane, and others babbled about nothing. The patients in the lockdown ward were definitely disturbed both mentally and physically. After having been bumped and pushed and my cane snatched away, I expressed my fear and concern—and was assigned a sighted aide 24-7.

On the first day in "lock down," Scott Purdy came to visit. He needed a plumbing diagram to install a gas water heater with a circulating pump. I asked for a piece of paper and pencil and proceeded to draw a very specific diagram of what he wanted. Gina was there when Scott came, and both were amazed at the accuracy of the schematic. For a moment they thought perhaps my sight had returned. Unfortunately, it had not.

On another day, life-long friend Charles Hancock, his brother Bob, and Pastor Jim from the Walden Baptist Church visited. It was as important to me to have spiritual healing as well as fine doctors and modern medicine. Prayer is very important and nurturing.

Each morning we patients would go to group therapy. On the second day, when asked by the lead psychiatric physician how I was doing, I told him I would be doing a hell of a lot better getting away from these people who had serious mental issues. After forty-eight hours, I was released from lockdown and taken to a more open psychiatric ward where I was free to walk the halls, go to the activities room, and not be in fear of people grabbing at me, getting in my face, and being confrontational.

I learned that my blindness was a minor thing after hearing the stories of the other patients. There were several women who had been abandoned and left with children. They had no self-esteem and tried to harm themselves. One had stabbed herself multiple times with a fork, some had over-dosed on pills, and others had used razor blades to mutilate their bodies. I was the "old man" on the floor and they were very kind and caring, guiding me to my room, to the activity room, and to the bathroom. When afternoon snack time (comprised of sandwiches, beverages, and ice cream) came, they would see that I got whatever I wanted. They were very kind to me, even though they were nuttier than I.

Patients played pool in the activities room. One time I asked if I could try. I took a cue ball and a numbered ball. Using my left hand to find the corner pocket, I pulled back about a foot onto the table. Using my cane as a stick, I knocked the cue ball into the numbered ball and it went into the pocket. The residents razzed me about pretending to be blind. On the second night, they were playing again. I asked if I could try a shot at it. Again, taking a cue ball and a numbered ball, lining it up with the corner pocket, and moving back, I used my cane as a cue stick. Not only did the cue ball hit the numbered ball, but the numbered ball hit another numbered ball. Each ball went into corner pockets. They swore that I was not blind and would not let me play anymore.

I saw a psychologist only five times for fifteen minutes per session during my stay. She was dismayed that I wasn't grieving in the clinically identified five stages of grief: denial and isolation, anger, bargaining, depression, and acceptance. I just simply accepted the fact that I was blind. There was no denial. I realized that I would be blind and everything that could be done had been done to save my sight. I wanted to go forward with my life. I need to learn how to live independently and wanted to be taught. It was hard to feel self-pity and wallow in self-indulgence when my two brothers, Robert and John, were dying a slow and torturous death from Huntington's, when my father had been burned alive along with his dog, when my older brother survived triple bypass in his early thirties, and harder yet to grieve in a "clinical" manner knowing the heroic deeds that the doctors had performed in saving my life.

When I got home, this is what Ann Gallagher, my social worker noted:

> Client does not feel that his stay in the hospital improved his mental condition. However, this worker notes that in the sessions they have had since he has been home from the hospital, client has been more emotionally stable. Also, client is thinking more about what he could still do as a blind person, rather than thinking there is nothing at all that he can do now that he has lost his vision.

I had told Ann earlier that I felt I was in a box of ice and I couldn't get a grip on anything to pull myself out. As I worked in the following months with my therapists, I found the rope I needed to get out of my despair. Prior to going blind, I had completely gutted the third floor of my building and had materials sitting up there ready for me. In a moment of pure madness, it occurred to me that finishing that apartment would be my rope. And so I began my new life.

Once you learn how to die, you learn how to live. It has been a key thought with me ever since I woke up from the coma. I think it has given me the impetus and strength to live.

7. Rehabilitation

This chapter is about my own rehabilitation and what has worked for me. I want to make it clear that my experiences may be different from those of other blind persons and that the opinions expressed here are my own. I hate the word "disabled." I am not disabled. I just can't see.

Rehabilitation really started while I was still in the hospital when I was finally able to stand and have a little mobility. My sister Rosemary was roundly criticized because she would take me out in the hall, give me a stick, and call to me from the other end of the hall. I would have to make my way past numerous obstacles to get to her. Then I would be put in a wheelchair and returned to my room totally exhausted.

After about four weeks of being blind, I talked to the gentleman from the Commission for the Blind and inquired what services were available. I will never forget that he asked me what I did before going blind. I told him I was a plumber. He said that with proper training I could go back to doing some plumbing. I said to him, "What?!! Are you out of your fucking mind?" I never dreamed that

I would be picking up a wrench or doing some plumbing which I loved to do. Yet within five years I was installing toilets and faucets and doing other types of plumbing jobs. All I needed was someone to hand me the right tools.

Rehabilitation is not a one-time training. After the initial rehab, there was still much to learn. I had to learn to perform a multitude of tasks. I had to adapt to day-to-day living. Each task was a mini-rehab. At times I had to be my own trainer. Other times I had coaching.

I learned how to adapt my home so I can turn on the heat or air-conditioning, how to do laundry, how to approach the kitchen and lay out where my food and utensils are, and how to use the stove safely. I have to organize where everything goes. Everything must have a place and be in its place. If something gets moved, it takes me hours to find it. When other people try to be helpful and put things away, it is often in the wrong place. I've learned it's easier to wash and put away the dishes myself.

When I modified my home after going blind, I installed all one-way light switches so that "up" always turns the lights on and "down" turns them off. That way when company leaves, I can go around and check to be sure all the lights are off. I modified the kitchen so that it is wide enough to maneuver from one counter to the other. The cabinetry is laid out for easy access to frequently used items. Many simple kitchen tools allow me to prepare something to eat. I had roll-out draws installed so that I can feel the contents and know what I'm touching. I modified my bathroom with such things as grab bars in the shower. I laid out the bathroom so that the tub, the sink, and the toilet are all in a straight line. I made all the rooms wheelchair accessible. The furniture layout and the choice of furniture was also critical. For example, carpet runners are not just runners—they are reference points that tell me where I am.

I had to learn how to arrange my clothes. I have a walk-in closet. All of my day-to-day wear is on the right. My dressier clothes are on the left. The shelving in the closet is sectioned according to the type of clothing: suits in one section, dressy shirts together, and trousers follow etc. I shop for everything in neutral colors so I can mix and match. My dresser is sectioned like the closet. There is a place for tee shirts, underwear, pajamas, etc. I can't look out the window and see what the weather is, so I have to listen for the weather report in order to choose appropriate clothing and judge whether or not it is safe for me to go out. Certain times of day, I make sure to wear something that is highly reflective so that I can be spotted by drivers. I have two pairs of identical shoes that feel alike but are different colors. I also have boots. I needed to find a quick way to identify the pairs and to tell the right boot from the left. I put a stick-on bump on the right heels of one pair of shoes. I know the shoes with the bump are the lighter brown pair and the ones without the bump are the darker pair. I also put a nylon wire-tie through the loop on one of my boots so I can easily tell the right boot from the left.

The most valuable piece of equipment a blind person has is his cane. The cane is my eyes. When I use it properly, I do not walk into telephone poles, fall into holes, or hit buildings. I learned how to use my cane for mobility outside of the house. Every person makes adjustments to the basic training. I was taught that there are two ways to use the cane. One is to leave the tip on the ground, sweeping back and forth in order to find small items that could trip me. The other is tapping. This is for rough surfaces such as grass, snow, or ice. If I move my feet, I must move my cane. When I cross a street, my practice is to move it vigorously back and forth to get the attention of drivers. They are more apt to see the cane than they are to see me. When approaching an intersection and hearing a vehicle coming, I put my cane across my body to let the driver know that I am staying stationary. The cane speaks to me in three languages. One is when I feel it strike something. Another is as it vibrates from tip to handle alerting me to seams in sidewalks, curbs, or holes in the road. It lets me know what kind of surface I am on. The third language is sound. As the roller tip rotates on the surface, the sound changes as I get closer to a solid object such as a wall or building.

I find that a sixty-inch cane works best for me. At varying times, I have forgotten and walked away without my cane. Within moments, I realize I'm blind and I cannot move. A broken cane is a nine-one-one call for a blind man. People should not grab at a blind person's cane. It's like someone putting a hand over a person's eyes. Children often want to play with it. I have to insist they don't because it is not a toy.

I had to learn to keep my right foot stationary when I stop and talk to someone or wait for traffic. I must keep it firmly planted in the direction I am heading. If I lift that foot, it is virtually impossible to get back to the exact position I was headed. By keeping that foot planted, I know the direction I am going in. Before going blind, I knew to look left and right when crossing the street. Now I must look straight ahead so that I can hear equally the left and the right to alert myself that there is something coming

Personally, I have found that the wind and the sun are great tools to use for direction. When I first step out the door, I try to sense the weather. For example, one very still morning I sensed a slight breeze from the north. Later, several blocks from home, I got a bit turned around. I turned myself until I felt the chill of the morning dew on my face. I knew then that I was facing north. On a sunny day, I can tell direction by feeling on what side of my body the sun is, for it comes up in the east and sets in the west. Winter is a beautiful time of year until I have to go walking. Where is the sidewalk or the road? With a howling wind blowing from many directions, I cannot see with my ears. I don't walk far in inclement weather.

Some blind persons use a guide dog. I decided not to because the community that I live in is basically one city block. A guide dog would be of minimal benefit for the distance I normally travel. I don't use public transportation. The essential services I need are within walking distance and the community in which I live has no public buses or trains. Having been sighted for many years before I became blind, I am very familiar with the area. A guide dog is a working dog and requires a lot of maintenance. They are also very expensive.

I chose, instead, to have a small companion dog. I picked a miniature schnauzer to keep me company. I wanted a "pal," not a working dog. Charlie loves to sit with me in the recliner. He's fun to get on the floor with and play. He's a good alert dog. Because of his size, he's very portable. I can pick him up and carry him or transport him in a car. It's very easy for me to control him when I walk him. Most importantly, he gives me a reason to get up and get going every day.

I have to be prepared for emergencies. Whether it be a fire alarm or a fall, I must have a plan for what to do, whom to contact.

The doors to my home are always locked, so I must prearrange for emergency entry. I have given keys to the rescue, fire, and police departments and have told them where I would be located in the event of an emergency that requires me to leave my home. Currently that place is next door in the doorway of the post office.

Simply putting toothpaste on a toothbrush is a major achievement. It took me years to learn to put a small amount on the brush and not all over the countertop. Every day I learn something new. For example, one of the things I had to learn is what to do when out in public with a lady and in need of a rest room. It is impossible to find your way around a public bathroom that has multiple stalls and sinks. Many times my friend has asked a man entering a rest room if he would help me. This is rather humiliating. People have been kind enough to wait as I use the bathroom and take me to a sink so I can wash and then escort me back out rather than just abandoning me there. I always ask for a stall, as I am not sure of my aim using the urinal. Where there is a single stall bathroom, many times my lady friend will go in with me to show me where the toilet, sink, soap, and towels are located. When a man waiting to come in sees her come out before me, you can hear him gasp.

When people try to assist me, they really mean to help. If someone unexpectedly grabs me to assist, I have to trust. I have to trust others with money. I have to trust myself more than anyone else in order to have confidence in the decisions I make. If I am not tired by the end of the day, I have somehow done something wrong, because every movement requires thought. This is exhausting mentally and emotionally.

Money poses a problem. Coins are easy, but bills are more difficult to identify. I have devised a system. I purchased a wallet with multiple compartments. I put the bills in separate compartments. Some are folded. Some are placed with the fold to the right and others to the left. Singles go straight. I adhere to this all the time. That way, I know what the bill is that I take from my wallet. To this point, it's been a good system for me.

I use a seven-day planner for my medications. But there are many bottles and it is difficult to identify the bottles and know how and when to take the medicines. A mistake can kill me. Luckily, nowadays there are talking machines and bar codes. These let me do my weekly medicines by myself. They articulate what is in the bottle and how to administer it.

Rehab did not prepare me for housebreaking a puppy. That was one of the most physically and mentally challenging things I've accomplished. I had to figure out how to walk him, groom him, and not trip over his toys or his messes. If he got sick or made a poop mess, I had to be prepared to clean it. It was not a big thing. In the end, the unconditional love he gives me every day makes it all worthwhile.

Eight years after my initial rehabilitation, I took a refresher course. Christina, my rehab specialist, reviewed some fundamentals of simple meal preparation that she taught me many years ago. I had never felt confident enough to make use of the training and became reliant on eating out or on the assistance of others. I'm learning how to organize everything I need to prepare a meal within a safety zone so that I am not distracted by having to move about the kitchen finding what I need during the process. I'm learning to safely adjust the burners and deal with hot pans. I can now transfer food from the pans to plates and safely to the table. This sounds simple until you have to do it blind. For me, it was terrifying. Do I have the flame too high or too low, or are the eggs done? I have to conquer this fear in order to live independently. The rehab specialists not only teach the mechanics, but they also instill confidence. Now I feel more than confident about being able to prepare a meal safely if I have to.

I also have been equipped with the latest electronic devices such as a barcode reader. The reader allows me to identify food that I take from the refrigerator or pantry. I can also take it to the store with me and know what I am taking from the shelves. If someone brings me food or a present, I can put a barcode label on it by articulating with my own voice what the item is and be able to identify it at a later time.

The ever increasing advancements in technology not only enhance my ability to function on a daily basis, but also positively affect my emotional state. Years ago blind people were confined to their homes or facilities. The advancements have continued over the years since I went blind.

I thought my life was over when I went blind. I had no comprehension of what was possible and what the future would hold. I had to conquer my fears and learn to trust people. I was limited only by my willingness to learn and to accept help. For example, a friend of mine took me for a motorcycle ride. We went about thirty miles. The experience was exhilarating. I had absolute faith in my friend.

Rehab starts with the mind. My mind tried to replace the loss of sight with visual memories. I had to overcome the fantasy of the mind and face the reality of the moment. I have wondered if life is worth living. I have asked that every day and the answer is "yes." I deal with depression. It will probably be, there for the rest of my life. I have learned to control it with medicine and counseling.

Acceptance of my life-long level of depression was one of the hardest parts of rehab for me. I had to face up to the fact and deal with it.

One of the ways was obtaining a computer equipped with the Jaws program from the Commission of the Blind. Subsequently, the Veteran's Administration has given me new computers and updated the operating control program for Jaws. Jaws is a program that articulates as I type and reads aloud when I get books on CD or something is sent to me in an email format. I had never used a computer or written anything more than a plumbing bill. I had a lot of learning to do. This experience helped me immensely in my rehabilitation process. On March 17, 2004, I began writing this autobiography. I branched out into poetry and emailing. A friend of mine had noticed a creative writing class in Greenville and thought it might be a help to me. The hilarious part was when the cab driver took me to a seat and no one would speak. So I said aloud, "This is a writing class?" I think seeing a blind man come to a writing class was a shock to them.

The emptiness after my loss of sight is a huge cavernous void. Don't let anyone kid you; it is not easy going day to day trying to fill that void with purpose and meaning—but you have to try. An important aspect of my rehabilitation has been pushing myself to do things that I would never have thought possible in the early years of my blindness—such as plumbing and heating, creative writing, and renovating the third floor into a new apartment. People have had faith in my ability to do plumbing totally blind. I refer to the days when I do plumbing as "mental health days" because it forces me to use my mind. The satisfaction of the people I've helped lets me know that my life isn't over. I just need to change the way that I do things.

At my request, Christina Kendall, my Vision and Rehabilitation Therapist wrote the following personal recollection.

Several weeks before I met George, I was in a local restaurant and noticed a flyer announcing a grand Welcome Home party for George Knauer. I knew this name from my caseload list and judging by the party advertisement, he seemed like a popular character in the local community. When I eventually arranged to see George at his home, I have to admit I was curious to meet him.

Upon arrival at his home in Coxsackie, one couldn't help but stare at the extensive mural of Get Well cards that adorned the front entrance from floor to ceiling. It was quite a spectacle and I had never seen such an outpouring of support for anyone like that before, nor have I since.

George greeted me with friendliness and enthusiasm. He was surrounded by his close friend, Gina as well as his sister, Rosemary and her husband; all who appeared to be very supportive of him and encouraging.

George was ready to jump into his rehabilitation program right away. Anyone who knows George knows he doesn't like to waste a minute! Most of my clients prefer to meet with me once a week, but George wanted to meet as often as possible. We agreed to meet twice a week, two hours per session. In addition to my training, George would be taking several hours of mobility training to learn safe travel skills and use of a long cane. He would also be receiving several hours of counseling per week to address the emotional impact of his vision loss. Although George seemed to be accepting his sudden blindness quite well at our first meeting, I knew that some of the most difficult emotional issues lay in the months ahead when the novelty of his program wore off and the permanence of the blindness settled into his mind. Still, it was good to have someone willing to work hard and try to maintain as much independence as possible.

We started off with some instruction with basic tools: learning to use a talking clock, a signature guide, a liquid level indicator for pouring safely, and organizing and identifying money. George, who had never been in the habit of using a wallet, went out and bought a very attractive one that allowed him to separate and organize his bills and credit cards conveniently. We marked his appliance dials with raised markings. His microwave, stove and oven were all marked so that he could set them independently and so that he could survive in the event that the Sbarbaro Restaurant closed down unexpectedly! I was treated to some lovely lunches as George learned adaptive techniques for slicing, chopping, boiling and baking. Ah, the good old days at George's Café! His thermostat and washer and dryer were also marked so that he could set them accurately.

George learned to use a Voice Organizer for recording and accessing his appointments, phone numbers, and memos. He also learned the Braille alphabet for identifying items like his CDs. For an extra challenge, George learned to use an adaptive sewing needle and practiced some basic mending, although he confessed he wouldn't be advertising himself as a seamstress anytime soon!

The final step in George's program was learning to type on a computer keyboard. George was not confident that his plumber's hands would work miracles on the keyboard, but he looked forward to trying to enter the millennium with some computer skills. Week by week, drill by monotonous drill, George's typing skills improved. Eventually, he became competent enough to receive some tech training to further his skills. It wasn't long before George was emailing like a technological madman. This basic skill along with some further academic training, have allowed George to re-channel his creative talents that were so deeply imbedded in sight into wonderful melodies of thought and sound. I wish him much luck!

When I met George in June of 2002, he was just reeling from losing all of his sight overnight from a sudden illness. Although rattled, he appeared optimistic and gung-ho about starting his rehabilitation program. He was completely unaware of what sort of future he might have as a person who was blind and knew little, if anything, regarding services or products that would be useful to him. Most people do not. George seemed excited by small devices that helped with the little things in everyday life such as talking clocks, watches, markings that helped him adjust appliance dials accurately. He was interested in recording devices and learning the Braille alphabet. George never appeared to be in denial that his vision loss was permanent although there was and probably still is that smattering of hope that some technique or surgery will reverse the situation. Everyone should have hope, it's what keeps us going, but George did not seem to be living in a fantasy that it was coming back any time soon. I can't say that I detected anger from George about his blindness either although he did express some anger regarding certain reactions to his blindness in which he thought some people were trying to take advantage of him. Unfortunately, there are always some people who will try to better themselves on somebody else's weakness. The biggest emotional component that I observed with George was depression. It rarely left him completely dysfunctional, and he rarely missed a lesson with me, but there were times when cooking lessons became counseling sessions and learning Braille was put aside to confide fears. As George learned to type (a very new experience for him), he often wrote of dark emotions. It was a very cathartic experience to finally put feelings into writing although at the time, at first, I'm not sure how much he realized he was revealing or releasing. He described dark, lonely feelings of isolation and hopelessness and dread. At the same time, George plodded on through his various programs, learning new skills, experimenting with new tasks he never did when sighted, and had a few real laughs doing it all. Other health conditions sometimes exacerbated his loneliness and it did help that George had a strong social network of close friends and relationships. George completed his rehab program, in terms of independent living skills in about two years; meeting with instructors several times a week at his home. The emotional rehabilitation took longer, but gradually George's writings took on lighter, softer, more grateful emotions. The fears of daily existence faded away and a longing to really live became more apparent in his actions and poetry. George is always throwing himself into new experiences which always helps one look forward rather than falling backward. Whether it's designing a new apartment, adopting an active puppy, providing plumbing advice, or rejoining the adventurous world of dating, George breathes new life every day into a sometimes difficult and challenging world. But, I suppose he would have done that anyway!

Christina Kendall
Certified Vision Rehabilitation Therapist
February 2010

Also upon my request Ann Gallagher, Social Worker wrote her personal recollection.

When I first met George he was dealing with the very sudden and traumatic total loss of his vision due to a stroke. Initially, George seemed to be in a state of denial or shock, as he was not expressing normal or expected reactions to such a loss. George was stating that he was not angry or depressed. Anyone who has a traumatic loss of vision naturally experiences the stages of grieving (denial, anger, sadness, bargaining, acceptance). It was apparent that George was in a state of denial. Soon after this initial meeting, George began to display behavioral signs of a deep and persistent depression. He seemed irrational and hopeless about his situation. While these are expected emotional reactions, George was getting to the point where significant medical intervention for depression would need to take place. Counseling continued with George, and his depression worsened. Blind Rehabilitation is a team work approach where counseling, rehabilitation living skills instruction, and orientation and mobility are instructed to a person to try to address all of their needs. In order for a person to feel that they can live with the blindness, all of these services are generally recommended. George was receiving all of these services to try to help him regain some independence and to learn how to cope and live with the blindness. However, George's mental state continued to worsen to the point of a breakdown. George was thinking and behaving like someone in a very deep depression. Before George could admit himself to a psychiatric unit, he had an emotional outburst and took several pills. This appeared to be a suicide attempt, so George was taken by ambulance to Albany Medical Center and admitted to inpatient psychiatric unit.

In the months following this episode, George maintained that he was not trying to kill himself. He was in a highly irrational and emotional state when he took the pills and didn't remember a lot of the details of that day. George did begin outpatient psychiatric sessions with a doctor from the VA and took medication for his depression.

George also continued to see me for ongoing adjustment counseling. As time progressed George began to open up more and to fully express his feelings of sadness, fears, and anxiety related to his blindness. He went from being very independent, owning his own business, riding his motorcycles, etc. to feeling trapped in his own home. This overwhelming loss of independence and control over one's life takes a lot of time to heal from and to cope.

George continued to receive rehabilitation therapy for daily living skills instruction and orientation and mobility for independent travel skills. George was very determined to regain his independence and to continue to live alone and to have meaning in his life.

Through all his ups and downs, George's many friends and some close family were very supportive of him and his ability to persevere.

George also remained the primary caregiver to his two ailing brothers, who were suffering from Huntington's disease and both living in a nursing home. George continued to visit them regularly and I think he took a lot of inspiration and strength from his two brothers and tried to apply it to his own life.

As George began to slowly regain a lot of independent living skills, his mood and overall emotional adjustment also began to improve. The things that seemed to help George the most were to have projects planned or things he was working on. The main project he tackled was to renovate the third floor of his home into a brand new apartment for him to move into. This gave him a feeling of great accomplishment and excitement to be able to do a lot of the work himself and to be able to still do things that he enjoys.

George also began to explore learning computer skills and tapped into his creative writing skills. These new focuses helped George to realize that he could still continue to grow and develop and to enjoy activities he had never really explored before.

When my counseling came to an end with George, it was apparent that he had gone through a lot of personal growth and change. George learned that he could still be the same person he always had been, only he needed to do things differently and he needed to have a new focus on what would make him feel successful and complete in life.

I continue to keep in touch with George and he has been a mentor for many of NABA's clients. He is always willing to talk to someone who is going through what he went through, to try to help them to understand that they can get through this difficult time and that here is hope, as George is clear evidence of this fact.

Ann Gallagher, Social Worker
February 26, 2010

8. Blind Mice Plumbing and Heating

November 1, 2004 was the beginning of Blind Mice Plumbing & Heating. It started with a sink faucet that wouldn't turn off. This chapter is composed entirely of recollections sent to me by my "customers."

My First Customer - Leslie

Years ago, when I casually mentioned to my friend Vicki that I needed my kitchen faucet replaced, little did I know that I would be planting the seed for a new business to be known as Blind Mice Plumbing. When Vicki approached George about the job, he enthusiastically accepted—especially when he knew that he would have the assistance of two gorgeous females! In preparation for installation day, George advised me of what faucet to purchase and what tools to have on hand.

I was amazed that the minute George crawled under my sink he knew exactly what he was doing and completed the job for the most part by touch. Vicki and I had a nice chat while George did all the work. We merely stood by to hand George the tools and parts he needed. As George lay on his back under the sink installing the faucet so effortlessly, Vicki said George was probably faking his blindness and accused him of looking up her skirt! The successful installation of the faucet seemed to take no time at all, and if my memory serves me correctly, George charged me practically nothing for the job. (Hopefully he made up for it on his next customer.) George is proof positive of the saying, "I could do that with my eyes closed!"

Recollections from Anne

Over the years, I have been privileged to 'assist' George with most of his plumbing jobs, whether in his own home or jobs that he does as Blind Mice Plumbing. I have learned many things, such as how to clean out a clogged drain by unscrewing the slip nut that holds the trap lever under the sink, same for bath tubs, how to clean out the holes in a toilet bowl if water was flushing slowly.

When George first met my daughter, she felt confident and asked him about her burping toilet. George was down on his knees, turned off water flow, got rid of standing water, installed a new ball cock and adjusted the height of the water level—problem fixed.

I moved into a small house which needed to be completely gutted, new electric, insulation, and sheet rock installed. After completing renovations in the living room and kitchen, I wanted to do the same for the bedroom and bathroom. The former owner had put cedar shingles on the walls for an inexpensive way of decorating the bathroom. George came over, took his crowbar and started tearing down all shingles. I cleared away the debris. He then disconnected the electric lights over the sink. The room was then ready for the electrician to rewire, insulation installed and contractor to install sheet rock, new sink, shower, flooring, and closet.

The next room George helped me with was the bedroom. Paneling and sheet rock came down as George took a hammer to it and out the open window it went. He took a knife to the carpet, cutting it into two to three foot lengths and...out the window it also went. George only managed to put one hole in the hallway wall—which was quickly repaired. If I did not know better, I would think that he could see. He sees in his mind's eye and accomplishes what he sets out to do.

I have always been amazed when going out on 'jobs' with him. He knows exactly what has to be done, uses his hands and fingers to size up the situation and proceeds to complete the task.

I assisted when he worked on another job where he installed a new toilet, pedestal sink with faucet, drain and water supply; also installing a new electric hot water heater. George would ask for a certain size crescent wrench, or whatever tool and I would generally be able to give it to him. I'm still not sure of the different tool names but George was patient and got the job done.

In my own home, I had a burping toilet and upon going down stairs, George realized that the previous plumber (who could see) had not put the vent in the correct position. Up on a ladder George went, with a hack saw, another piece of plastic pipe, some glue, my assistance, and got the job done properly.

Another time, he changed out my electric hot water heater. I was concerned when he started to cut the copper pipes as to how he was going to reconnect them. Before coming to a job, George has all necessary parts and everything planned out in his head. He had couplings with which he connected the copper pipes. When reconnecting the electric, again I was not sure how he was going to handle that. As a blind man, he was working with two hundred twenty volts of electric and how was he going to know which wire went where. I was nervous but surprised when his knowledge of handling electricity paid off and everything worked.

George is not afraid of tackling a job. My two hundred seventy-five gallon oil tank needed to be cut with a saw-all. He had me insert the blade into the hole of the upright tank and told me to hold on to his belt, thus guiding him around the tank. The saw was vibrating so much that his silver bracelet kept spinning around his wrist. With the tank cut into quarters, he was able to carry the pieces up from the basement and outside for proper removal.

I was presented with a small white pipe wrench attached to a lovely wooden stand with a plaque "Plumbette 1st Class - Anne 2010". George has an imaginative way of saying Thank You and it holds many fond memories of a special plumber.

One day he was called over to Marie's home. Her grandson had flushed a sponge tooth brush down the toilet. The toilet had been bolted to the floor for many years and the bolts would not come undone, thus, reaching into his canvas tool bag (which he is never without), he pulled out a hack saw blade. The bathroom was narrow but he laid down on the floor and started sawing the bolt off. He is still amazed that when Marie's husband Fran came in and found a blind plumber taking apart his toilet that everything remained calm. He then removed the toilet, laid it on its side to remove the toothbrush from the bottom. George got the toilet put back together. Because of the age of the toilet, it was re-installed temporarily. A short time later, George removed the old and installed a new toilet. Another job was nicely done by Blind Mice Plumbing and his assistant—me. I'll let Fran tell you personally of his experiences.

Once again, Blind Mice Plumbing and Heating returned to help me solve another problem with my basement. My soap sink and washing machine were draining into what I thought was a 'dry well' but apparently it was draining into my foundation keeping my basement very damp and moldy. On day one, he came with a fiber optic camera to check out the drain and we found it blocked. Sizing up what was needed to correct the problem, he came prepared with PVC pipes, fittings, glue/cleaner and a self-contained transfer pump; and with the assistance of his 'plumbette'—me. Within one day, George had everything figured out and installed so that water is now going to the septic system instead of flooding my basement. Then we redirected the condensate drain into the new drainage system. Again, it is amazing to watch him handle his tools—almost as if he can see.

Fran's recollections

George Knauer had been our primary plumber for a number of years prior to his blindness, even after he tried to sell me a gold plated sump pump. Had I not noticed the gold paint in his fingernails, I probably would have gone for it!

Once Blind Mice Plumbing was formed, I was, admittedly, somewhat reluctant to continue with his plumbing service. My wife had no such qualms. I came home one day to find George sprawled on the floor of our four by six feet former pantry which is now a tiny bathroom. Our five-year-old grandson had tried to flush a toothbrush down the toilet. The bowl had to be removed, laid on its side in order to get the tooth brush removed from the underside of toilet. The toilet had been bolted to the floor for many years and the bolts would not come undone, thus, reaching into his canvas tool bag (which he is never without), he pulled out a hack saw blade. George's feet extended into the kitchen as he sawed off the rusted bolts. I was a bit concerned to say the least. I feared that at least one of his fingers would be severed, but this didn't happen. He removed the obstructing items from the pipes, replaced the bees wax seal, and set the toilet down on the wax insuring a tight seal. George does not avoid gook, slime, and grime which results in a very dirty mouse. Because of the age of the toilet, it was re-installed temporarily. A short time later, a new toilet was installed. George was aided by his 'plumbette helper'.

The second job George took on for us was at our new cabin. Both our upstairs and downstairs toilets, although new, were leaking badly. This time I, not my wife, called him. Each time I flushed the toilets, I had to turn the water off. He said: "I'll be glad to fix them for you." My question was, how is a blind man going to fix these toilets. After picking up the parts for the toilets, I picked up George and brought him out to the cabin. The downstairs toilet presented no problem for him, He took the water tank off the toilet, put in all new parts, reassembled the toilet and it stopped leaking. The upstairs job concerned me more as he had to walk up a narrow staircase and work in another small space. I need not have worried. The stairs presented no problem nor did the cramped space in which he had to work. He resolved the problem quickly and everything has worked perfectly since.

Another time, while a friend of his was putting in my new central air conditioning, George could hear the well pump clicking on and off, on and off. That led to finding a broken outside garden hose fixture.

I intend to use Blind Mice for any similar plumbing malfunctions. Thanks again Blind Mice Plumbing.

Thoughts from Glen

I prolonged the project as long as I can. We were in the house for 7 years already. Every other room had been touched and we just couldn't deal with the outdated lame excuse for a bathroom that our guests were using. The downstairs bathroom project had to begin. I can't say that I wasn't a bit skeptical when my wife suggested that I call George for some help. She'd spoken on many occasions about how he had over 30 years of plumbing experience. The thing I just couldn't figure out was how George could help. After all, he was totally blind. My personal experience with plumbing was very, very limited, almost non-existent, but for some reason the thought of getting help from a blind plumber made me feel extra incompetent. My wife had known George for several years and she repeatedly mentioned to me how resourceful and connected he was and how he always offered help with anything to do with the house. I finally relented and decided to contact George and take him up on his offer.

Before we called George and asked for help, my wife and I did the typical do it your self-er research and thought we knew what we wanted. When we called George on the phone to touch base on the project, I could sense the excitement and passion on the other end of the phone. He was more than willing to help out with whatever he could. A couple of days passed and we got a call from George "Stop over my place, he said, I made a call to my supplier and there's a catalog here I want you to look at". When we stopped by the next day and picked up the catalog, George said "Just give me a call when you've picked out your fixtures". A couple of days later we let him know what we wanted. He said "No Problem" I'll handle it from here. The next day we got a call from George and he said the stuff would be delivered in a week or so but we should stop by tomorrow because he ordered all the supplies you need for the project and I got his usual contractors discount. I didn't quite know what he had ordered.

My wife stopped by the next day and George told her to have me give him a call when I get home from work. When I got home from work and saw what he ordered I was totally shocked. There were boxes of supplies. When I called George, he immediately began to explain exactly what he ordered. "In one of the boxes you'll find a copper elbow and a toilet flange and a quarter-inch coupler and a ceiling fan and so on and so on. He did not miss a detail. He knew exactly what was needed to complete the entire job. George even picked up on two things that he ordered which were mistakenly missed by his supplier. OK, my confidence with the project was certainly growing.

I'd decided that I was going to do a lot of the "grunt" work myself. It took me a while to finish the rough plumbing. I made countless calls to George in a panic and each and every time he talked me off of the ledge and calmly described exactly what I needed to do. Nothing was a surprise to George when it came to plumbing. He basically talked me through every step of the process. Finally the rough plumbing, the sheet rock, and the tile were finished. In the meantime, the shower, sink and toilet were delivered to my house and were ready for installation.

The big day was here, I was planning on taking a half day off from work, George and I were going to install the sink and the toilet. Anyone who has remodeled a bathroom will be able to tell you how big of a deal it is to finally have your toilet and sink working again. My wife and I were excited to say the least. I was pretty nervous though. The last thing I wanted to deal with was an issue with the plumbing that George talked me through. The tile and sheet rock were already finished and all I could think of was the need to tear the wall down for something I messed up. George said that he'd be at my house around 2:00 p.m. with his "assistant"; my plan was to leave work at 1 to be there in time. I called home at 1:00 p.m. to let my wife know I was on the way and she said that George had showed up early and had already started. Oh my god, I thought to myself. I really wanted to be there! I sped home at lightning speed. My car was barely in park before I was out of the car and running toward the house. I entered the house and headed straight for the bathroom. I arrived to find George on his back on the floor under the sink with a wrench. He had already installed the toilet and was just finishing up the sink. I was in utter disbelief. In about one half hour the sink was finished. Everything worked perfectly, without a drip. George went on to tell me that he'd decided to order a hot water mixing valve to hook up to my toilet so the cold water in the toilet bowl doesn't produce condensation on the outside of the bowl in the summer and drip on the floor.

About a week or so later George came back to my house and installed an electric hot water heater, which he gave to me. He ran a line to the floor underneath the toilet and hooked up to the hot water mixing valve that was tied to the toilet.

George certainly exceeded my expectations. Who in their right mind would have thought that an individual who is blind can be such a capable plumber? He's a master plumber by his own right and a great friend. Not a week goes by without me thinking of what a great help he was. Everyone who comes to my house has nothing but great compliments for my bathroom and I share my experiences with George with a good many of them.

Little does George know (until he reads this little excerpt) but I'm planning work on the second bathroom this winter and he's sure to get a call from me.

And here's, the rest of the story:

Would you believe I actually decided to start the second bathroom on schedule. Partly due to the pressure from home but mostly because of my new sense of confidence with plumbing (thanks in no small part to George). Every time I walked into the grungy lame excuse for a bathroom all I could think of was how I wished that I'd chosen to use the 'other' bathroom. You know, the one with sparkling new fixtures and fresh smelling paint. I knew that I would have all the support I needed from George with one phone call so I decided to make the call. George sprung into action immediately, as expected, he made contact with his supplier. Within days I had several catalogues from which to choose our fixtures and shortly after that the order arrived at my home. Just like bathroom number One, the order was complete with nearly every single elbow, washer, faucet, etc. Basically everything I needed to complete a full renovation of the bathroom. I found myself far more competent in bathroom number Two than I was the first go-around. I'm not going to lie though. Not a day went by when I didn't have to call George and have him talk me off the proverbial plumbing ledge. George demonstrated considerable patience as I peppered him with question after question, scenario after scenario. Nothing was beyond his abilities to comprehend and lend solid advice and instructions. I'm sure he struggled on many occasions to understand the crisis of the moment I was trying to describe but he was always able to weed through the words, always asking the right probing questions and honing in on the right guidance. Everything was looking great. The day finally came to put the cherry on the top of the cake. Of course I'm referring to the throne. George had highly recommended that we purchase a toilet with an insulated bowl and some other bells and whistles and that's what we had ordered. This time I made sure that I was there to help with the installation. George led the effort and in no time we were good to go.

I often stand back and admire the two bathrooms that I remodeled. I learned a great many things about plumbing and myself during the projects. However, the most memorable thing I took away was all about George. His passion, knowledge, dedication and friendship is an inspiration to me. He has helped me to truly understand that you are who you want to be. Embrace what you have (disabilities or otherwise), make no excuses and most importantly help your friends along the way.

It happened just the way it always did for us. Right in the middle of the coldest part of the winter; yet another home crisis involving one of the basics of normal living. Hot water, you can't be without it for long. Our hot water heater was on the blink. That's all I knew. As was usually the case with such a crisis, Blind Mice Plumbing was my first call. I was pretty sure George would have no trouble diagnosing the issue over the phone. That's what I'd come to expect. I described the problem to George over the phone and without hesitation he said "Turn the breaker off that controls the hot water heater, remove the cover from the top access panel of the tank and push the red button. If you feel the button snap then you are probably good. Then turn the breaker on and you should hear the sound of water starting to fizzle as it heats." I followed the instructions and was extremely pleased to find that all was well again. I never even knew that red reset button was there. Crisis averted, or so I thought. A few weeks went by and life was good, as far as I knew. The water was hot and I only needed to reset the button once more. My wife had the opportunity to speak with George shortly after and she happened to mention that I had reset the button once again. George showed immediate concern at that point. He mentioned to my wife that it was dangerous to reset that button a second time. Apparently it was a sign of a bigger issue with the hot water heater that could cause a fire. A day or two later George had the replacement water heater in hand and within forty-five minutes of starting the job George had the old tank removed and the new one installed. The new tank was purring like a kitten; no offense meant towards the Blind Mice. As the old tank sat in the garage awaiting its drive to the dump George had one more suggestion, which he made by phone the following day. He had deduced the apparent cause of my troubles was hard water and a build-up of deposit on the elements. George instructed me on how to remove the drain from the bottom front of the tank, which I did. He told me to stick my finger in the hole and take note of how much residue sat at the bottom of the tank. It was up to my first knuckle. I relayed that information to George at which time he recommended a yearly flush of my hot water heater to clean out the hard water deposits, which should greatly reduce the likelihood of having similar hot water troubles again. Thanks again to George; a plumbing challenge was quickly and skillfully resolved. With a new hot water heater in place we were ready to tackle the colder than usual Northeast winter and I actually learned something too. Although there is a reset button on your hot water heater you should only press it once.

Reflections on My Encounters with Three Blind Mice Plumbing And It's Proprietor - by Victoria

Was I crazy? Or adventurous? Or just cheap? (I mean, how much could a blind plumber really charge?) I prefer to maintain a positive self-image; I'll take the "adventurous" option.

So I saw, one fine early summer day, George the Plumber standing on the street. We had spoken before. I worked up my courage and inquired about his availability to lend me some plumbing assistance. We arranged a day and a time. He informed me I would be his assistant.

OK, back to the crazy/adventurous/cheap theme. I will admit to being a little well, not crazy, but perhaps ummm, a bit different. But then, I reasoned, anyone who is completely blind and persists in plying his trade as a plumber has to be a tick or two off the norm also. Adventurous? Absolutely...how could I resist giving Three Blind Mice a try? Cheap? Well, as a single parent supporting a teenager and a lovely, demanding Victorian house on a teacher's pay, economics must play a role in my decisions.

There's more to it than that. I was impressed by George's demeanor. He spoke with confidence and intelligence. His experience in the plumbing field was obvious when we discussed the jobs I needed done. My farming background had taught me that a person who is smart and hard working (George fit the bill on both counts.) can accomplish a lot, even if a few obstacles get in the way.

So over the next few months George and I cooperated on several jobs. My kitchen faucet got correctly installed. The environmentally unfriendly garbage disposal met its maker. A leaky, reluctant diverter valve was replaced by a stylish new tub faucet with a smoothly functioning valve. The drip in the basement was mended. George knew what he was doing, and he knew how to work within the skill set he currently possesses while drawing on his years of experience in his profession. He was patient with me as his assistant. In a short while, I was promoted to the level of "Plumbette".

In the course of our adventures in home repair George and I got to know each other. We found out that he and my mom had something in common—the orphanage experience. We shared lots of laughs as our conversations ranged from politics to popular culture to philosophy. I was and continue to be impressed by the many interests George has and his array of talents. From the beautiful photographs he took, to his skill in writing, to the renovation of his building, George's determination and desire for creative expression take many forms.

I very much appreciate having the opportunity to get to know George. If you know anyone who needs a good plumber, or a good writer, or a good partner in conversation, I will gladly recommend Three Blind Mice Plumbing and its Proprietor.

Reluctance. It's what you expect from an eight year old who is ordered to bed on a lovely, still-light-out summer evening, or a teenager made to emerge from slumber land at 7:00 a.m. on a weekend. It's not what you expect—or want—from your toilet. But it transpired with my downstairs commode in the middle of winter. I gave it a week to correct itself. No deal. It was time to call Three Blind Mice Plumbing. George came over. We snaked, we plunged, and finally, we pulled the toilet out and worked around the other end. This is a delightful way to spend a winter's evening. George reinstalled the toilet and ran a few tests with paper and flushes. It seemed to be back in good working order. George is, of course, the Blind in Three Blind Mice (I have yet to find out about the mice.). Somehow he was able to do all of the above plumbing work with minimal help from his assistant, me. We did have a nice time talking. He told me a story about recovering a diamond ring from a toilet. It had an inexplicable jingle as he removed it from a customer's home. A few moments with a hammer uncovered the ring, stuck in the mysterious folds of toilet topography. Back to reluctance. It returned to my toilet within a day or two. The final option was upon us. Replace it. George ordered me a toilet and we spent another midwinter's afternoon removing and installing. As a grand finale, we brought the old toilet out into the yard, applied a few sharp blows with a hammer and...mystery solved. Not a diamond ring, alas, but a pen. Yes, a pen, stuck somehow so it acted like a baffle, allowing water to flow past, but precious little else. This, my friends, is NOT what you want a toilet to do. When is it time to call George? That is the question that plagues me. George, amiable fellow that he is, usually can fit me into his schedule rather quickly. I, on the other hand, am hemmed in by work and childcare and the myriad of other chores that face a single parent. Having a sweet, large, old house to maintain doesn't help.

The drain stopper in the upstairs bathroom was getting more difficult to operate every day. I couldn't avoid the issue any longer. It was time to call George. He explained to me that it could be a pretty easy fix if all went well. "IF" being the operative word in this situation.

Due to commitments on my part we had to get to the job on a very hot day...in May. May, when the weather is supposed to be lovely; a pleasant interval between the unpredictable spring of upstate NY and the sun and heat-filled summer. On this day, a betrayal of May's promise, the temps climbed to 90 and kept on going—perfect for crawling around on a bathroom floor, right?

George was his usual equable self. He didn't complain, he didn't throw a wrench at me or the wall. I could not have blamed him if he did (well at least at the wall), because the IF made its presence known on this job. Most of what could have gone wrong did, including me dropping the drain plug down the drainpipe. We had to remove the pedestal sink...a new skill to add to my "Plumbette's" repertoire.

It was also interesting to watch how George approached the job of reassembling the drain. His memory must have served him well. To me it was a rather confusing contraption. But he said to me that it was simply like a puzzle, and you had to fit all the pieces together in the right way. Congratulations, go out to him. He solved the puzzle. Then came the fun part: We had to remove the old drain. This was to be accomplished by George. He squeezed into the alcove by the sink on his back and, wielding a skill saw, attempted to cut the pipe. I have always been impressed by George's plumbing acumen and his ability to defy the limits of his impairment, but I tell you now, folks, you have not lived until you have seen a blind man jammed into three foot square space using a two and one-half foot saw twisting whichever way possible to cut a pipe.

Life is long and holds many an interesting byway. I think I

passed one of them this May. My great thanks to George and his mice for their help and their stories.

Well isn't it like life to take you from one extreme to the other? Several months after the hottest-day-in-May incident, I called upon George's skills again. My fuel oil tank was in the process of being replaced, a cold snap popped into our area with flawless timing, and I needed help draining the fuel line to keep all members of the household from freezing. George talked me through the entire process over the phone. He also patiently guided me through the many steps that would be involved in getting the new fuel system installed.

I have come to count on George, not only for his plumbing skills, but for his calm leadership in a crisis. How many people would amiably explain what to do when someone (yes, yours truly), calls after 9:00 p.m. on a brutally cold night because the thermostat just broke? He offered to come up and work on it himself, further evidence of his kindness. Fortunately, his description of what to do was so clear that I didn't need to drag him out in the cold.

Most recently George installed a new faucet in my bathroom sink and removed an old dishwasher. As usual, his phenomenal competence manifested itself. He knew exactly what to do in both cases. I assisted only by handing him whatever tool he needed. Bravo to George and Blind Mice Plumbing!

"Where Does the Water Go?"

An aspect of life that few laypersons take time to contemplate, but plumbers spend their working lives dealing with, planning for and resolving issues about is wastewater. Hence, where does the water go? Unless you live in a drought-prone area it probably goes down the drain, never to be thought of again. Some drain, some-where. A fact about life: if you have plumbing, you have drains.

George has helped me out with drain situations many times. We have snaked toilets, moved pedestal sinks to get into tight spaces hiding drains, and figured out earth-friendly ways to speed up a reluctant exit of water from the bath. Each and every time George approached the job with confidence and know-how born of years of experience. When we need items, we visit the local hardware store, where he is greeted by name. No one blinks or raises an eyebrow when he reels off a list of the plumbing supplies he requires for his current job. Then he is off to the rescue, saving people from too intimate contact with the much maligned and abused wastewater.

Thoughts from Kevin

It turns out a blind plumber beats me in a handyman contest every day of the week. After having (again) run out of healing oil and failing at the time-honored task of bleeding the fuel line to get the boiler running again, my options seemed to be few. Bleeding the fuel line again seemed pointless, and waiting for a conventional plumber seemed out of the question. A cold front was due, and my family was not willing to tolerate more cold showers.

My wife strongly suggested that I do something. By which she meant get some help, and she meant George Knauer, who had been her landlord and our friend for years. "But he's blind," I said. "Maybe he can walk you through it," she said.

So I made the call, and George tried valiantly to walk me through the process. But I failed him. As I searched my mind for alternatives, George rasped, "Just come pick me up." So I did.

George came with his own tools, organized to a tee, so that he wouldn't even need me to hand him the tools. He worked quickly and neatly, explained what he was doing, and a few minutes later, started the furnace. He left only a half cup of oil for me to throw back in the fuel tank.

I don't know how he did it, but even blind, he's a better plumber than I am. I learned a lot that day, and not all of it about plumbing.

Thoughts from Louis and Loretta

It is amazing what a blind person can do. When the oil company said we needed a new gauge in the oil tank, they wouldn't change it. So we called George who got right on the phone; ordered the part and we went to pick it up. Then picked up George, brought him to our home and he proceeded to remove the old part. It wasn't an easy task, but he got the job done and put the new part in. Never under estimate what a blind person can do.

Thoughts from Nancy

My friend, George Knauer, has been blind for some time, but in spite of his blindness, operates very successfully I might add, a plumbing and heating business called, "Blind Mice Plumbing and heating". George and I have been friends for a couple of years now, but haven't seen each other for quite a few months. I emailed him on Saturday to see how he was doing and mentioned to him that my kitchen sink was leaking like a sieve. He immediately offered his help, said he would come over on Monday to fix it. Fixed one pipe that wasn't even connected and readjusted and tightened all the fittings, and was all finished in under 20 minutes. If I had hired another plumber, I'd still be doing dishes in the bathroom or running dirty dishes over to my daughter-in-law's home to wash them for another week or two at least. All he wanted for payment was a coffee and a bagel. When you have a friend like George, you have a friend for life. Thank you George

Thoughts of Three Blind Mice, Arthur Jack Knauer Jr.

In 2009, I was in need of a new boiler. My brother George Knauer, was a licensed plumber who had many contacts but as the Heading says, due to an accident on the job he lost his eyesight and is totally blind.

I asked George, because of his contacts, to find a new boiler for me. He and I worked together installing this new boiler. Since his blindness, he has let nothing stand in his way; nothing would stop him from installing the boiler. And what could go wrong, he's only working with natural gas, water, and electricity.

Now mind you, he can be hardheaded, meaning that he pushed me out of the way most of the time and continued to replace the boiler. He and I worked on the boiler for approximately 5 hours.

Of course as brothers, we argued about this and that. Never the less, with his touch, feeling each part, he installed the boiler. As I said in the beginning, we argue about everything. To my surprise, when we were done, the boiler was up and running. I was surprised, by his tenacity not to give up on life and go forward with the work he's has always done.

On top of all of this, he has so far written five books. He writes poetry, sometimes you can see the darkness of his blindness through his works. Nevertheless, he has won awards for his writings. He has not let his blindness stop him from doing what he wants.

I can totally tell you, that if I was in the same position that I could not do what he does. My hat is off to him and so should yours.

Thoughts from Josie

In the summer of 2015, the post office had a plumbing problem in the men's room. The urinal wasn't flushing properly and emitting a smell. We called a local plumber to analyze the situation.

He arrives on site and determines that there's a blockage in the pipe and that the urinal was "starving for air". He then asks me if I happen to own a plunger, after looking at him in awe, I say, "you're the plumber!, don't you have a plunger in your truck?!, we don't have children here to shove anything down the pipes, we're working adults." He instructs me to call the local septic man to snake the system, and leaves.

At this point, I knew it was time to call on the neighbor for a second opinion. George was over immediately to assist and said, "There's no blockage! He ordered the parts that needed to be replaced, and immediately got to work fixing the problem. It's a pleasure to have a knowledgeable man to call on for the job. We appreciate his expertise and quick service in fixing our plumbing problem. He is amazingly talented in his profession, thank you George for your wonderful service! And yes, he is totally blind.

9. The Flight of the Tidy Whiteys

Late one night,
My life took flight.

Out of a window I did fall,
From a great height.

Unlike a bird in flight,
I did not soar so well.

It wasn't the fall that bothered me at all,
It was the sudden stop that was a shock.

AND HERE IS THE REST OF THE STORY:

On Monday, July 31, 2006, four and a half years after suddenly becoming blind, I was still suffering from debilitating nerve damage to my left leg. I called the pain management clinic at the VA Pain Clinic begging for something to be done. They gave me an appointment. When they saw me, they decided to give me methadone. With this medicine, the pain greatly subsided. I was told to take it three times a day. Two days later, I phoned Anne around 10:30 p.m., concerned because I had moved some furniture but did not remember doing it. I knew I was disoriented, but I didn't associate this with the methadone. I thought that I might have taken a too much of my regular medications. She came down to help put things in order. I had moved my bed, bedside table, curio cabinet, and dining room chairs. The next day everything seemed to be okay. We went grocery shopping and did several other errands.

On Friday, August 4 I went to a scheduled visit at the pain clinic. They wanted to see how I was tolerating the methadone. As everything seemed okay, they increased it. However, while waiting in the pharmacy for pills, I started sweating profusely. By the time Anne and I got home around 4:00 p.m., I was vomiting and became increasingly disoriented. I called the pain clinic, but they had already left for the day. Next, I called the pharmacy and mentioned that I was having "hot flashes." I could tell the woman on the other end had covered the mouth piece and was laughing with her co-worker over a man having hot flashes. She probably should have told me to go to the Emergency Room. Instead, she told me to stop taking the methadone since I only started it on Monday.

On Saturday, August 5, 2006, I was to have gone grocery shopping with Anne but was not feeling well. She started out on her own but returned when I telephoned her. I was having trouble keeping food down and was vomiting. I think the methadone must have still been in my system. When Anne came back, she cleaned up the living room and bathroom. I rested while Anne headed out again. After returning with groceries, I was able to help her put things away. She fixed me a sandwich and went home.

That evening, sometime around eleven, I got up to open a window to let some in air. I think I tripped over the leather office chair near the window. I may have grabbed it in an attempt to support myself as I reached for the window. The chair was on casters and may have skirted out from under me. In any case, I lost my balance and out the window I went. My only thought was, "Oh, shit!" You know how your mother tells you to always have on clean underwear when you leave the house? At least when the emergency services people arrived, I had on clean tidy-whiteys and one slipper.

I had fallen head first out the third floor window, past the screen, and very, very luckily landed head first in the awning (over the first floor offices) before continuing down to the sidewalk. One of the Coxsackie police officers shook my right shoulder and asked if someone had pushed me or if I had fallen. I don't remember answering.

Anne got a telephone call around 11:00 p.m. Saturday night that I had fallen out the window. When she got downtown, she saw the broken awning and the crowd that had gathered. I had already been transported by this time so she then drove up to the hospital.

I had few broken parts, but I was alive and at Albany Medical Center. Gina and Anne got there while I was in the emergency room. Around 5:00 a.m. I was admitted. After I was settled in, Anne left me. I had fractured the upper part of my left femur, both sides of the pelvis, and T1 in my neck. C1 and C2 were also damaged. I'd been on Plavix, a blood-thinner, so the doctors were unable to operate to put a steel rod in my femur. They had to wait a week for my blood to thicken.

Anne came back Sunday night and told me there was crime-scene tape stretched across the front entry to my home. Monday morning I was alert enough to phone the police to see if it was okay for Anne to enter my apartment. Officer O'Brien said he would meet her there. When she returned to my apartment on Monday morning, they looked at the room from which I had fallen. They concluded that I had probably been supporting myself on my computer chair while trying to open or close the window, some-thing that I do daily. Apparently the chair, which swivels, became unbalanced and turned over. I must have reached forward to the window sill in front of me where my hands landed on a towel. The towel lay on glass covering the windowsill. I had put it there for Max, Anne's miniature Schnauzer, to catch the warmth of the sun when he visited. They figured the towel must have slid forward and away I went.

Several days earlier, I had heard that there were going to be gusty winds and asked Anne to roll up the awning. It extended five feet, and luckily, instead of rolling it up completely, she left it extended about two feet. Someone was just coming out of Blue Water Bistro, a restaurant across the street, and heard a thud. They almost ignored what they heard thinking it may have been a bag of garbage or something that had fallen. They investigated anyhow, saw who it was, and called nine-one-one. Whenever my name is called in, the local Fire and Rescue Squads and the police hustle to get to me (as I was a long-time member and used to help out by driving the ambulance when I wasn't at work.) I was picked up in no time and on my way to the Emergency Room at Albany Medical Center. I do not remember hitting the side walk or talking to people when in the ambulance, although they said I did.

The next day Marie De Francesco came to visit. She had been working with me on this book for a little over a year. As she bent over to give me a kiss, I became startled. She thought I would have recognized her perfume as she approached the bed. "You didn't have to go this far to get another chapter into the autobiography. This is carrying it to the extreme," she teased.

On Monday, August 7, the doctors said that they had to drill a hole through my leg to insert a temporary pin to put me in traction. Being blind, I just couldn't wrap my head around the idea of a hole being drilled in me. Once again, Rosemary and her husband Guy stepped up when it counted. I was also shocked and surprised, to find many years later, that my brother Arthur Jack Knauer Jr was also in attendance. They came that day, however, because of the extent of my injuries and being heavily medicated, I was unaware that they had come and helped communicate my medical history with the doctors. They were able to keep my friends Anne and Gina up to speed with what the doctors were planning. My oldest sister Kathy failed to show. I was not bothered by Kathy's absence in my two life-altering situations, but I was devastated when she made no effort to attend the funerals of Robert and John. Guy is a retired X-ray Technician and was able to explain how badly I had fractured my pelvis in two places and shattered my left femur. The pin would go through the bone beneath my knee to keep the fragments of bone from touching and prematurely knitting before the steel rod could be inserted. As a contractor, I was interested in the tools that they were using.

Anne had previously arranged to visit her sister in New Jersey. On Tuesday, August 8, there was no reason for her to cancel her trip as I was in good hands. When she got to New Jersey, she phoned me and later told me that I was not making sense with my conversation. The medicine had taken its effect.

When Anne returned on Friday from her visit, she came to see me around 2:00 p.m.. When the nurse asked what my pain level was, I replied, "Three." That was the first time Anne had ever heard that number. Usually it was nine or ten because of the pain that I had been experiencing since my stroke and blindness. I contribute that "three" to the fact that the doctors had me on a good amount of pain killers. The doctors told us that I was on standby for surgery on Saturday.

Anne came early on that morning to be with me. By 11:30 a.m., we were on our way down to the basement operating room. By 3:30 p.m., I was in recovery and back in my room around 5:00 p.m.. Gina and Anne had been in the waiting room all this time.

The next day when the nurses and doctor came by, they noticed that I could not feel their touch on my left foot and took me down to have an X-ray. They discovered severe nerve damage in my foot. It was over a year before most of the feeling returned to that foot.

On Monday, less than forty-eight hours after the surgery, two burly women came into my room and snatched my ass out of that bed. They put a belt around my waist and forcibly stood me up. Although the bulk of my weight was on them, each movement was very painful. They showed no mercy. I figure they must hire the meanest, toughest people they can find to do this kind of job. They sat me in a wheelchair and took me over to physical therapy where I began some basic treatment.

Physical therapy was rough. By the time they got me out of bed, I was in so much pain that I could hardly function. The therapist showed me how to tie a long rubber band on my left foot and pull on it to help stretch the leg's muscles.

When I graduated from Jell-O to solid foods, I faced a new problem. It was most uncomfortable to have a bedpan shoved under my ass. To make matters worse, I could not tell if it was going to be flatulence or solids—a hard situation to be in when dependent on others to move your body.

Being blind had been a bit of an advantage when I fell out of the third floor window because I couldn't see the sidewalk rush up to meet my face and I wasn't panicked, but now in the hospital my blindness caused me a great deal of anxiety because I couldn't see what people were about to do to me.

I remained in Albany Med until the eighteenth when I was transferred to Eden Park rehabilitation facility in Catskill—just ten miles from my home where friends and family could easily visit. During my stay at Eden Park, Anne arranged for my barber, Richie Bruno, to come and give me a haircut. I hadn't had a haircut in at least two months. He took ten pounds off my head which helped me feel much better. He brought another visitor with him, Tommy Deyo, another local plumber. We'd often cover for each other when one of us was on vacation. He had recently unintentionally ended his plumbing career as I had, by accident. An unsupported staircase had fallen on him, so he understood what I was going through. There were many other friends that stopped over or phoned. Their thoughtfulness helped make my confinement much easier, and I thank them.

I began rehabilitation on August 22. With the help of aides, I was able to get out of bed and sit in a Brody chair and be taken to physical therapy. My pain medicine had been increased and my Foley removed, so I was comfortable and functioning. Michelle had me hopping with my right foot while holding the walker in addition to using four pound weights to do arm curls. (When she asked for ten curls, I did fifty.) I felt very good being able to do the physical therapy. However, by evening I was in excruciating pain. Physical Therapy had not received all of my records and they did not realize that my pelvis was fractured on both the right and left sides and I should not have been hopping on my right leg.

Dr. Phelan, who operated on my leg, saw me Monday for a standard post-operative visit. X-rays were taken and things looked good. However, I would still have to stay off my left leg for about eight weeks. I originally thought that only a short rod had been inserted into my femur, but when my friends saw the X-Ray, they told me that a full-length rod had been placed inside the whole femur from my hip to my knee.

The doctor who had treated me for the fractured vertebrae in my neck also took X-Rays and told me I would need to continue to wear the neck brace an additional month. I would need a follow-up X-Ray before I could take it off.

I was not happy at Eden Park. Aside from the damage done to me in physical therapy, the isolation was getting to me. I was given my meals in my room and only found out next to the last day that I could have gone to a central dining room and the activities room. The beds were either too soft or too firm. I found out that they had given me the wrong type of mattress. I left the nursing home because I seemed to have fallen "through the cracks." Twice, an evening nurse refused to give me the pain medicine the doctor had prescribed. She thought that I might go into convulsions. Meanwhile, I could not get to sleep because the pain from the injuries intensified. I could not see spending one hour a day in Physical Therapy and the rest of the time isolated with nothing to do except watch TV. I decided that it would be in my best interest to go to my own home. I could practice my physical therapy during the day on my own. I could shower in my own tub. There is nothing like sleeping in your own bed. It would also be more accessible for visitors. In any case, under the Veteran's Administration rules, I could only stay there twenty-one days.

I called the captain of the Coxsackie Rescue Squad and said, "I need a ride home. Get me the hell out of here." The Human Resources Officer at the nursing home said that if I left, the facility would see that I did not get home health assistance from the county. I told him that the second I left there I was going to contact my lawyer about the poor physical therapy and rehabilitation services that I was enduring. With that comment they changed their minds and made arrangements for the services of The Eddy to follow me home. They then called and verified my statement that the rescue squad was going to transport me home and not allow me to walk up the thirty-three stairs. Once a wheelchair and walker had been secured from the VA and arrangements made for the services of The Eddy for physical therapy and nursing care, I was allowed to go home.

I checked out of Eden Park on Wednesday, August 30. Anne came early that morning to learn how to put my new support stockings on to prevent blood clots from being in bed for so long. When I heard the voices from the crew of the Coxsackie Rescue Squad, I felt wonderful knowing that I would soon be home and in good hands. Anne got to the apartment before I did and had the doors opened and entry way cleared. The stair chair that they transferred me to was heavy and with my weight (even though I had lost eighteen pounds) it took four guys to get me up the stairs. Being a part of a small community is wonderful. When times get tough, there are people there that you know personally and it is comforting. I went home and it felt fantastic being in my own bed and in my own home. I felt part of the community again. A physical therapist came twice a week and gave me a good work out. He assured me that once the doctor gives me the okay to stand on my left leg, I would be walking by Thanksgiving. Meantime, it was quite a challenge to maneuver the wheelchair with my leg out straight and no sight. Transferring from the wheelchair to the toilet or tub was comical. It allowed me to laugh at myself.

I arranged to have a ramp put in on the back porch so that I could be wheeled outside and enjoy the fresh air. It was nice to have meals out there and hear the noises of the community. Anne, Gina and I enjoyed dinner out on my back deck over-looking the Hudson River. Although I cannot see the beauty of the park and river, it is wonderful to be able to enjoy the air, sounds of children playing in the park, and company of my friends.

Getting around my home in a wheel chair, I began to realize how my brothers Robert and John must have felt in their many years of being wheelchair bound. Rod, the physical therapist from The Eddy, showed me how to get into my shower with the new shower seat. When you have the right equipment and are shown how to use it, life can be much easier.

My friend Gina offered to assist me and came over at 9:00 a.m. each day before she went to the office and helped me put on my support stockings and assisted me in whatever I could not yet do for myself.

Gina and Anne took turns spotting me as I transferred from the wheelchair to the shower. They were "Peeping Toms." I got the wheel chair parallel to the tub, and took off the left foot bracket and the left arm of the chair. Once this was done, I could put one leg at a time into the tub and slide off of the wheelchair onto the tub seat. Fortunately, prior to the accident, I had already installed safety grab bars which were invaluable in making the transfer. The first time I got into the shower and changed the water flow from tub to shower—WOW it was COLD. I learned that the hot water has to be turned on to be warmed up before getting in.

Life continued with the routine of getting up each morning, getting into the shower, shaving, and getting dressed. My wardrobe consisted of pajama bottoms and a tee shirt. They were comfortable and easy to get into. After dressing and having breakfast, I went to the living room and started doing my physical therapy exercises. There were days that I could do a full routine, but other days I couldn't. I was determined to be able to walk as soon as possible. If I had energy left, I would check my e-mail or do it in the afternoon after a nap. My routines left me tired, but I knew and could feel that my body was healing. Rod came back once a week to see how I was progressing and was pleased with my progress and some-times would alter the routine. I found that he had been the physical therapist for several of my friends. He seemed to know what he is doing, and I had a lot of confidence in him.

Early in September, I invited Peggy and Hugh Quigley and Vickie and Gerard Ecker for dinner. They had been very good friends, and I wanted to let them know how much I appreciated all their help. Anne set a beautiful dining room table and prepared a lovely dinner. It was great socializing because visitors were rare and the months were long. On that occasion Anne took care of making sure the lights were on. That didn't always happen when I had guests. Many times when people came, I would simply forget to turn the lights on. Central Hudson, the regional power company, once questioned my usage as they thought with such low usage I was doing something illegal.

In mid-September I was introduced to the use of a walker which allowed me to support my weight, be more independent in moving, and not rely so heavily on the shoulders of Anne or Gina. I continued to be concerned about the swelling in my left leg. Rod felt that it was okay and that I should still continue to wear the support stocking. Either Anne or Gina put it on after my shower. I was finally able to bend my leg more and could get it off by myself later in the day.

At this time I agreed to have a monitor from the Eddy Life Line program installed. I had put off from signing up with this type of program because I felt it was an "old fogey's device." However, since falling over in my wheel chair three times, it now seemed that the Life Line program is to my advantage. Once I touched my necklace, the beeper on the monitor would go off, notifying the alert center. I then would have the opportunity to speak with them. They could hear my voice from every room in my apartment. If they did not hear me, they would notify the local police who had a key to my home and would respond quickly. It turned out to be a life-saving piece of equipment. One time I had a choking episode in the bathroom and passed out. I must have pressed the button because Gina and Anne showed up and rescued me. Another time, when first using my walker, I came out of my bedroom and tripped on a runner carpet and as I began to fall, I grabbed for the desk chair. Unfortunately, it swivels. After slamming face-first into the wall and knocking myself semi-conscious I was unable to find my walker or crawl back to bed. Again, I do not recall pressing the button, but within what seemed like moments, two police officers were picking me up and putting me back to bed.

By mid-September I was getting back into some familiar routines. Marie De Francesco, a retired English teacher who had been working with me on my autobiography along with Anne Foster, a retired Post Master, resumed work with me on my autobiography. My days have been busy with exercises and therapies, but I really missed doing my regular routine of walks, visits, going out for breakfast, and being able to go where I want to go.

I was able to laugh at falling out of the window, believing that I would overcome these injuries as I had overcome many other obstacles. I realized that it would take a lot of work on my part. However, Dr. German, the brain injury specialist, had told me that there are things that might happen to my body that I would have no control over. He had explained that after trauma to the head, blood can start to seep and collect on the brain. If this occurred, there would be a noticeable change in my speech, thought process, and movements as well as vomiting. I was a little frightened about my recovery. Although frightened, my choices were still the same: either to maintain my physical therapy so that I could walk again or to sit and do nothing which was not a viable option.

I went to see Dr. Phelan, the orthopedic surgeon, for a post-op visit. The pain in my lower legs was intense. He assured me that everything was progressing fine. He explained that in addition to the rod being inserted into my femur, five pieces of wire had been wrapped around the bone for additional support. There was some nerve damage done which was causing the pain in my lower leg. He also informed me that a screw that he had used to secure the rod in my femur to my knee had broken. He showed the x-rays to my friend Anne and, for once, the world had confirmation that I really do have a screw loose. What followed were five surgeries and a shiny new knee.

I had an epiphany: my falling out the window and having bones broken was not for naught. I realized that I went on a CRASH Diet—losing 27 pounds. Take it from me there are a lot better ways to go on a diet.

Dying really is not the problem. It is making it permanent that bothers me ☺

CPSIA information can be obtained
at www.ICGtesting.com
Printed in the USA
FFOW02n1428210416
23403FF